THE POETRY GAMES

South Coast Counties

Edited by Mandy Robinson

First published in Great Britain in 2013 by:

Remus House
Coltsfoot Drive
Peterborough
PE2 9BF
Telephone: 01733 890066
Website: www.youngwriters.co.uk

Book Design by Ashley Janson

SB ISBN 978-1-78203-509-1

Printed and bound in the UK by BookPrintingUK
Website: www.bookprintinguk.com

Foreword

Since our inception in 1991, Young Writers has endeavoured to promote poetry and creative writing within schools by running annual nationwide competitions. These competitions are designed to develop and nurture the burgeoning creativity of the next generation, and give them valuable confidence in their own abilities.

For our latest competition The Poetry Games, young writers from across the country were given the challenge to stand up for what they believe in using nothing but the power of the pen. Using poetry as their tool, these aspiring poets were given the opportunity to express their thoughts and feelings on the topics that matter to them through verse.

Whilst skilfully conveying their opinions through poetry, the writers showcased in this collection have simultaneously managed to give poetry a breath of fresh air, brought it to life and made it relevant to them. Using a variety of themes and styles, our featured poets leave a lasting impression of their inner thoughts and feelings, making this anthology a rare insight into the next generation.

Contents

Moira House School, Eastbourne

Oaklands Catholic School, Portsmouth

Osborne School, Winchester

Peacehaven Community School, Peacehaven

The Leigh Technology Academy, Dartford

The Priory Coxlease School, Lyndhurst

Wilmington Grammar School for Boys, Wilmington

THE POEMS

Sorry

Sorry.
One short word,
It can mean so little,
It can mean so much.

Sorry.
Two syllables,
It can draw a beginning,
It can draw an end.

Sorry.
Three tenses,
The sound of regret,
The sound of hope.

Sorry.
Four constants,
The bringing together,
The falling apart.

Sorry.
Five letters,
From a true heart,
From a calculating mind.

Lucy Scullard (14)

You Know Who You Are

You make me feel small when I am big,
Up in my face, the tears then fall, I wondered why you're screaming in front of all.
You make me feel weak when I am strong,
Intimidation follows me everywhere, people may stop and stare.
You make me cry when I tell myself I won't,
Voice like a siren singling me out, my heart beats faster as I race, as you shout.
You make my heart fill with sadness, what have I done?
Screaming all the names under the sun, presence like a lion upon birds.
You make me feel I'm in the wrong,
Can't everyone see the jack in the box, although it jumps without being wound?
You make me feel scared when your presence is there,
Aggression devours you, you are one.
You make me long for what I feel I have missed,
A figure, an influence, and a guardian gone.
You make me wish I could never forget your name, but I still think about you all the same,
Do you care? Do you wonder as I do? Or am I all you said I was?
You make me angry, I wonder why,
But most of all I'm angry at myself, for letting go I may need some help.
You may linger in my mind, but never will you receive forgiveness in my heart this has fallen apart.

Georgia Walker (15)

History Poem

History . . .

Events roll the tiles of time,
We pass through day and night.
Seasons come and go,
Empires rise and fall,
Fortunes change hands.

We witness periods of prosperity,
We witness periods of suffering,
We fight wars and battles,
We reconcile and agree.

As we aspire for a better world,
Time creates our history,
Time makes us relevant,
Time makes us irrelevant.
It teaches us who we are,
It re-makes our fortunes and future,
Fulfilling the promise of the Supreme Being.

History is a reminder that nothing lasts forever,
History is always in the making.
One of my favourite subjects in school is history,
Because history is always a mystery.

Jenny Liu

What's Peace

I speak through eloquence even though some are ashamed of intelligence
Getting brainwashed by the rap stars, being filled with ignorance
While the government send soldiers off to profit from the unconscious
I take my stance and start to meditate
I hallucinate, a place where I can locate
Peace, where there's no bombs left to detonate
Where we work together and all sit at the table and have a full plate
A place where there is no hate left for us to regurgitate
Let's start to change because this world we live in is slightly deranged
Kids go to school, pass your exams and see how life turns great
I read books and gain knowledge consistently
I don't encourage people to transgress and party
Instead I provide knowledge to make them think about life instantly
Cos there's too much poverty, diseases and sickness
Spreading constantly leading to life in misery
Ain't it funny how no one likes to be unique
Just want to copy what they see on TV
Wearing skinny jeans trying to be a G
Following the crowd like mindless zombies
That's why there'll never be peace in these London streets
They say kids are the future
First let's reverse our ways and dream like Martin Luther
If I were in power I would unite the people to build a better world.

Aziz Osman (17)

The Attack Of The Wasp Man

Me and my friend were going to play football
When we saw a wasp's nest which we thought was kind of cool
My friend kicked the ball in the tree with glee
Out came the wasps in a swarm, attacking me!
What a transformation in just a few hours
I became Wasp Man with strange and amazing powers
The next thing I knew, I was flying above the River Thames
When I heard a girl calling my name
She shouted, 'Help!' as she began falling off the clipper boat
I shot down to the river and grabbed hold of her coat
My wasp muscles came in handy
As I dragged the lady into safety.

Dillon Coster (13)

Watch The Time

People with happy smiles pass me,
I'd forgotten how to do that simple gesture,
Their thoughts are likely happy too,
Mine only hold guilt and gloom,
They wear watches,
I'd forgotten about the time,
Now I hold guilt and gloom,
It's too late, she's gone,
Now I hold guilt and gloom.

Aimee Whitmee (14)

My Mum

Your eyes shine bright like the stars at night.
Hair like waves on the raging sea.
Your smile like a dream.
Voice like the singing angels.
A temper like a thunderstorm.
A heart like glistening gold.
Skin as pale and the feathers on a dove.
Lips red like the petals on a rose.
Eyes brown as the leaves in autumn.
Although all this has gone, you're still in my heart, for evermore.

Chloe Short (13)
Amery Hill School, Alton

Africa, Africa

Africa, Africa,
It's an amazing place,
Africa, Africa,
It's falling at a pace.

We need to save this continent,
Or else it will be gone,
We need to save the rainforests;
Deforestation is wrong.

Most people in Africa,
Are starving to death,
Drawing closer to the underworld,
With every breath.

We need to do something,
To keep this place alive,
We need to do something,
For animals to survive.

Africa, Africa,
It's an amazing place,
Africa, Africa,
It's falling at a pace.

Annie Freeman (12)
Amery Hill School, Alton

Some Typical Days

On one snowy, summer's day . . .
I shot into bed,
And put on my clothes.
As I fell up the stairs,
And ate up my milk,
I unwashed my face,
And put off my gloves.
As I met with my friends,
And made snow-cubes,
We got back inside,
Dry as a bone,
Since the snow we played in,
Turned out to be foam!

But on one sunny, winter's day . . .
I went to the beach,
Not by car,
But by bear.
I made castles with water,
And washed in the sand.
I ate lollies with cones,
And ice cream on a stick.
The heat made me cold as a brick.
I bought an inflatable,
The size of the sea,
I guess some sailors weren't so pleased with me.

My upside-down story . . .
Has come to an end,
Or is it better to pretend,
That this is just the beginning?

Katie Mason (12)
Amery Hill School, Alton

The Forest

The forest,
My friend.
He whispers to me,
Weeps when he is sad,
Calls me at dawn.
The rustle in the forest trees,
It comforts me.

Winter is coming,
Icing sugar dusts the forest's floor,
Chilling my soul,
Lonely – yet so alive.
Dazzling balls of glittering air,
Flying past,
Brushing against my face.
The dry, chapped skin separating from me only reminds me of winter.
The departure from the crisp, crackling leaves,
Winter is coming.

Twittering birds,
Wiggling worms,
The lime green and emerald sea.
Twigs regaining strength,
Pathways revealing length,
Spring is on its way.
Glistening dew droplets drip,
Drip down to the forest floor,
Nourishing the earth,
Filling me with glee,
Spring is on its way.

Shining beams,
Light bending through the luscious trees and woods.
Children laughing,
Water splashing,
Glistening diamonds,
Swimming grace.
Weather is blissful,
Sorrow – abysmal,
The joys of summer dawn on my being.

But now all fades.
The desperate screams of the wind,

Hollow my thoughts,
And now, I don't believe things I used to.
What if there was no plan to life?
What if the wind disguises a secret?
What if the breeze lifting your spirit
Is an old, abandoned soul, trying to reach you?
So close,
Yet so far.

The forest,
My friend.
He whispers to me,
Weeps when he is sad,
Calls me at dawn.
The rustle in the forest trees.
It comforts me.

Olivia Welch (12)
Amery Hill School, Alton

My Best Friend

My best friend, she's beautiful
She's so stunning like a waterfall.
Her eyes are hazelnut brown
And best of all she never frowns.
I wish she knew how amazing she is,
She walks with a spark and a little fizz
She's lady-like every day
And is confident in every way.
I admit we've had our ups and downs
But we just forget and laugh out loud.
I remember yesterday she threw a mint at my brother's head,
I swear we'll never recover from it! (Because we laughed so much!)
She sets herself a goal and reaches it.
And usually I teach her it. (Her goal I mean)
So at the end of the day, when there's nothing left to say
Except I love her in every way!

Alisha Frost (11)
Amery Hill School, Alton

Endangered Animals

Polar bears are losing their homes due to global warming,
Jaguars are dying out at a rate that is alarming
Rhinos are being killed for the horn upon their head,
Something needs to be done before too many animals are dead.
It's happening to animals both big and small,
From elephants standing so big and so tall,
To a tiny little ant that just carries around a leaf,
The rate at which they're dying is almost beyond belief.
The cutting down of rainforests is a massive way,
That animals are being killed every single day.
They'll lose their homes and shelter and their source of food
And we humans just barge in there, it really is quite rude.
Poachers are killing the animals just to make some money,
It's mean and cruel and horrible, and I don't find it funny.
Killing a poor animal, just to make a profit,
When in reality, we really should just stop it.
There is no need to kill them, when there's so much we can learn.
Because with these beautiful creatures, that's more worthwhile to earn.
To understand their species, I don't see why,
Any single one of them should have to die.

Rebecca Wood (15)
Amery Hill School, Alton

The Old Grey Man

The old grey man.
Bends now at the waist.
He grasps the air with his fingers,
But catches nothing.
His toes drill into the ground like corkscrews,
Down, down into the sodden soil.
His wounds are covered in sap.
Yet he still stays the old man of the forest,
Proud and wise.

The old grey man.
Watches his children's perfect peach blossom drift gracefully down
to the ground.
His green trousers keep him warm through the winter.
His skin is peeling and rigid.
His hair turns from green to brown and then drops,
Before growing back the following year.
Yet he still stays the old man of the forest,
Proud and wise.

Emily Coates (11)
Amery Hill School, Alton

Story Of My Life

I'm searching for a book,
But I don't know where to look!
Where is the letter A?
'Miss! I can't find my way!'

She shows me the place,
Books stacked in a case,
I step into the story,
In all its shining glory . . .

The rustle of the pages,
Like opening some cages.
A book is wild and free.
This is where I want to be.

I'm landed there,
In sadness and despair,
Everything's wrong,
It's worse in the long run.

Lots of things here,
Enough to shed a tear,
I just hope,
That they can all cope.

Will it work out?
I'm full of doubt;
But love binds us together –
The very strongest tether.

Without love we would die,
And that is no lie;
Because, after all,
We are all mortal.

The library in my head,
Shows me that love isn't dead.
It's the story of my life,
So it will have to suffice.

Hannah Stone (13)
Amery Hill School, Alton

What If?

What if I hadn't minded?
Been easier to persuade?
Maybe she'd have been happy,
To stay in my shade.

What if I hadn't yelled?
Despite what she'd done?
Maybe she'd still love me,
Father, daughter, one.

What if I'd been home?
As she arrived back each day?
Maybe she would have told me
The problems in her way.

What if I'd hidden those pills?
The ones for my pain
Maybe she wouldn't have swallowed
And stepped out into the rain.

What if I'd found her quicker?
Waiting for death in the wheat.
Then she wouldn't be lying,
Down here, by my feet.

Emma Hughes (12)
Amery Hill School, Alton

In Memory

Your eyes were like a dream
Your soul was ever so meaning
Your heart beat like a shooting star
Your voice was so precious, glowing
Your heart. I could see all of those things in your heart Grandad, but this poem is just for you to remember how much I love you.

Maisie Webber (13)
Amery Hill School, Alton

How Does Man See The Beginning Of Time?

How does Man see the beginning of time?
Gazes at Heavens, wond'ring from whence he came,
Celestial objects, their orbits sublime,
Moon, in her beauty, she doth wax and wane,
Newborn stars, under cloud of ether bright,
Ancient comet, trace your eternal path,
Magnified by eye of glass; gather light,
Sirius rises, dog days here at last,
Pegasus, drunk on moonbeams, stretches wings,
Ursa Minor tumbles through Milky Way,
All time, reflected in a crystal lens,
Hidden in plain sight, all Man's answers lay.

Artful mirror peering into deep space,
Doth ponder questions of the human race.

Laura Denton (14)
Amery Hill School, Alton

Wolf

We are free as the Earth and the sky,
Roaming the land we live in packs.
Frightened of the human beasts that try,
They try to take us with their horrid acts.

Our eyes are as beautiful as a breeze,
Our paws skim lightly across the ground.
We howl as the moonlight hits the trees,
Our cubs dance joyfully at the sound.

We are the wolves and we are free.

Emma McInally (13)
Amery Hill School, Alton

Cowards And Heroes

While cities burn and armies turn
To flee in disarray,
Cowards cry, 'tis best to fly,'
And fight another day.
But soldiers know it's in their bones
When they die and fall,
It's better to have fought and lost than
Not have fought at all.

Matthew Fordyce (13)
Amery Hill School, Alton

Great London

If only you knew, what happens behind the London Eye.
The aftermath of the Olympics, the story behind the riots.
Greater London.
Our Great London.
Stood tall amongst the ages and rock solid throughout our wars, only to be brought down by our very own.
You who prise, your rise of the realm, look down upon those who aren't at your level.
You sneer at those who insult your intelligence, yet you foolishly judge those of street knowledge.
And you.
The youth of today, always trying to be something you're not.
Even another race, run your mouths as you run away from the stereotypes of black.
Asian. Labelled as aggressive, gangster, street urchin for race.
Never shall you hear of those who remain content without their 'chariots', if you knew what happens behind the London Eye, the story behind the riots.

Morenike Garber (16)
Beechwood Sacred Heart School, Tunbridge Wells

It's All Going Too Fast

It took nine months to wait for me the dread,
That must have caused,
From the talking, the screaming, the shouting,
And soon after the pouting,
Mascara, eyeliner, foundation and all,
I love it but my mother can't keep up with it all.
The nights out with friends makes my mother go round the bend,
She hates it, she hates the fact her baby is gone!
But I always say, 'I'll always be here Mother,
I'll be here through 'night night' and dawn!'

Mia Fiore (12)
Beechwood Sacred Heart School, Tunbridge Wells

The Day I Ended Up In A Prison Cell

It was my birthday today,
I was going to turn twenty,
But one thing to another, led me into a prison cell.

I was out partying on a Friday night,
I was really drunk and didn't really know where I was at the time.
I shouldn't have taken it . . . But I did just to impress my friends,
I didn't think it through,
I thought it was a cigarette but I was wrong.

I foolishly decided to walk home with the cigarette in one hand a beer bottle in the other.
A police officer passed me . . .
He stopped me . . .
He searched me and found a little bag
He arrested me . . .
Then the next minute I woke up in a cold, damp, depressing cell
Wondering what I had done.

Vincent Tang (14)
Beechwood Sacred Heart School, Tunbridge Wells

Alcohol

Drinking can be fun,
But you've got to think about when you're done
Drink some wine and have a good time
But when it comes to the vodka don't be a plonker
Think about your liver,
It could be getting thinner.
Think about your liver,
It could be getting bigger.
You think you'll be cool,
But you'll look like a fool,
And you can't stop thinking,
About drinking and drinking.
Spending all that cash,
Irresponsible and rash.
What would your parents do?
Well let's just say they won't be happy with you!

Lucy Whitehead (14)
Beechwood Sacred Heart School, Tunbridge Wells

Smoking

Smoking why do it?
Think of the harm it does your body . . .
Causes heart attacks
Burns your lungs black!

Smoking why do it?
Some people say it's bad, some say it's not,
Just don't listen
They think they look cool,
But they won't look cool when they're dead!
So don't smoke it's all a joke!

Thomas Warburton-Smith (13)
Beechwood Sacred Heart School, Tunbridge Wells

A Wolf's Life

As structured family of intense loyalty,
Faithful companionship striving for a future of prosperity,
Howling for a pathfinder,
Howling only on the full moon,
It's always travelling,
Always for so long,
It gets so tired,
But wait how could it ever forget about its food,
A dark shadow,
Under the trees like brooms,
Gleaming yellow eyes,
Watching its prey's every move,
Pounce: there it goes,
There was snarling, snapping and sadness,
Finally it has finished devouring its lunch,
And it runs away from the discarded bones,
'Owooo!'

Esme Ray (12)
Beechwood Sacred Heart School, Tunbridge Wells

Tough Love

A back hand slap against my thigh,
With the pain spreading like a dark night sky,
Expecting another as I hold the tears in,
But fall to the floor, as the punch flies in
Face against the floor, I realise is there any point living anymore?
The tears start falling as he walks out,
I ran upstairs as I heard him shout,
I thought you loved me, but I guess I was wrong . . .

Anna Smith (13)
Beechwood Sacred Heart School, Tunbridge Wells

Lone Wolf

Lone wolf, striking figure,
Howling on a hill.
Silhouetted in the moonlight
While all the earth is still.

Earlier, running through the forest,
Didn't even know it was there,
But alas it's too late,
He's caught in the hunter's snare.

His pack are far away,
Oblivious to his cries.
He just can't pull his leg out,
No matter how hard he tries.

Exhaustion takes over,
Now realising he's on his own.
He thought his teeth were sharp,
But the steel jaws have sliced to the bone.

Digging deeper and deeper,
It's impossible to bear,
Howling to the full moon,
But his family just aren't there.

Lying down on the ground,
Now all he can do is pine.
At last he closes his eyes,
For the final time.

Lone wolf, ghostly figure,
Howling on a hill.
Silhouetted in the moonlight
Can you hear him still?

Millie Smith (12)
Beechwood Sacred Heart School, Tunbridge Wells

The Futile Circle

Waking up craving,
Uncertain of the new day,
Doubtless to be like the day before that,
And the day before that,
Slipping away from problems in hand,
Unable to face up,
The solution lies in the liquid,
The source that makes you run from all that is right,
The emptiness it carries, desolation.
One more, you promise to yourself and another.
The addictive cycle that shuns the real world,
The world that holds your complications,
Blind to your fatal weakness,
Drinking more and more
The darkness closes in,
Out like a light,
But wake up craving.

Francesca Hayes (13)
Beechwood Sacred Heart School, Tunbridge Wells

Adventure

The adventure begins,
When it wants to begin,
It twists and turns,
And from the adventure you can learn.
The exciting adventure always turns,
Into a disaster made by her,
Magic and mystery coming today,
Turn around, it's on its way!

Here it comes,
The adventure is here.
The adventure in the sea,
Is made just by little old me.

Lucy Fawcitt (11)
Beechwood Sacred Heart School, Tunbridge Wells

What The Brain Said To the Lung

Cigarettes, cigarettes they make me thrive,
They are the source that keeps me alive,
If I don't get a cigarette I will feel like a pile of dung,
The brain said to the struggling lung.

Please, please stop,
I can't take any more,
I am beginning to wonder if there is any point living anymore,
Isn't this addiction a bit lame,
The sad lung said to the brain.

I can't stop I'm sorry,
It's something I can't avoid,
You must be so annoyed.

I don't have the strength to be annoyed,
I'm dying,
Didn't you realise,
I'm under so much strain,
The weak lung said to the brain.

OK, OK I'm addicted,
Now I have killed you,
I will be next,
The dying brain said to the . . .

Lucy Clark (13)
Beechwood Sacred Heart School, Tunbridge Wells

Why Am I Here?

I've been fighting in the war for weeks,
It hasn't been productive,
I have shed many lives, oh I feel rubbish,
I've seen my many great friends die,
O it brings tears to my eye.

Why am I here? I have done no good,
I should be at home, I really should,
Why am I fighting I have no idea?
I should be with my family where there is no fear.

Bombs, grenades exploding at will,
My head is damaged I need a pill,
Gunshots, aeroplanes up ahead,
They're coming to attack, I'll be dead.

Jolyon Ward (13)
Beechwood Sacred Heart School, Tunbridge Wells

One More

Can I have one more, one more?
I want to be blissful again
No more tears, I'm so full of fear and I don't want it ever again.

Please just one more, one more,
One drug will do no harm
I just want to see what I saw before.

Give me one more, one more
And I'll be fearless again,
Once I've got it I won't let it go,
Just one more please.

I just had it, one more, one more I had,
I felt vibrant after that few more,
I'm in that happy place now,
I'm here and not coming back,
This sleep it feels so good.

Ellie Hartong (14)
Beechwood Sacred Heart School, Tunbridge Wells

Who?

Who sends the beasts dark at night?
But ultimately wants you to be alright.
Who conjures the monsters to haunt you
And dreams of wealth to taunt you?
Who speaks to you in your voice
And guides you in making your choice?
Who controls the fear, suffering and pain
But makes you proud, happy and vain?
Who makes you fierce with pride
But forces you to run and hide?
Who teaches you right and wrong
And finds a place where you belong?
Who will make you laugh and smile
And who will take you that extra mile?
Who? It's you.

Harry Higgins (16)
Beechwood Sacred Heart School, Tunbridge Wells

Getting Home

I'm scared, scared to go home.
Cup of tea, dinner ready,
But something's not right.
She scared me I'm afraid.

Walking through the door.
Quiet as a mouse, I try.
She sees me.
I've been spotted, trapped.

I stand there listening.
Listening to the abuse, seeing the abuse and feeling the abuse.
The breath of alcohol in her.
I'm scared to call her my mother.

Fred Axworthy (13)
Beechwood Sacred Heart School, Tunbridge Wells

Love

For you it means light,
For me it's a burden.
This heavy weight on my heart
There for all to see
Is a warning. Take heed and fly,
But I cannot, it is too late for me.

They come in the night,
Their faces dark,
They come for me.
They take all I care about;
And they burn it.
It's a sign, a sign they are coming.

Gun in my back, I walk.
People screaming everywhere,
Then a place, a grinning place of grey and white
A shout, 'God save me,
Does this faith cause the end?'
Too late I realise. It was my cry,
A single shot.
Then I hear no more.

I worshipped you,
I loved you,
But this love is what killed me,
It is your star that caused the end.

Alexandra Williams (15)
Beechwood Sacred Heart School, Tunbridge Wells

The End

Blink, blink, blink.
I fall.
Blink, blink, blink.
The fading.

Commotion around me, but silence,
I crumple to the ground,
I see my life flash before my eyes,
My childhood, my youth, my non-existent adulthood.

My school, the people, the place that ruined me.
The death of my mum, the fall of my dad.
My sunken, swollen, staring eyes.
The things I stole, the things I took, the things I paid to scar me.

Who would think?
The place, that saved me would be my end.
The day I signed up, the day I got my boots.
They have been with me through all of it.

Back to now the end of my war,
My friends I've lost, I will see them now.
This will be the end of my suffering.
The end.

Alice Hedley (14)
Beechwood Sacred Heart School, Tunbridge Wells

Day Trip; That Changed History

We had spent months saving, planning,
This day has kept us going through,
The year, the hard times and the good.
We awoke early determined to make a change.

The four of us sat, some excited, some nervous,
We had been delayed, held back. All had become tense.
Our leader, the father of
our pack, held us, kept us calm while we awaited arrival.

Sitting upon our seats we awaited the signal; take off.
This time was my first time, this time I will hold my nerve.
I held the seat tight, sweating, hand in head,
Then the shout came, roaring down the seating area, fear reigned over.

Lying down upon the floor some screamed, some silenced.
Shouts slithered down from the cabin, then a sudden change of direction.
I stood a child in prayer waiting, wishing.
All I had ever wished for was a holiday away from our home, America.

My father's shouts rained down, mothers held their children close, partners held their loved ones together, then a blanket of silence folded down . . .

Bullets flew, people hid in the little cover they had, and my father, a hero, ran down the aisle, drinks trolley in hand and through the door. It was over.

We could feel the plane dropping, dropping down towards American land.
Fields of American crops, American happiness, American hope.
A place I now look down upon.
A place I am proud to call home.

Bailey Horler (13)
Beechwood Sacred Heart School, Tunbridge Wells

Bullying

They tear you apart,
They get in your head,
They shatter your heart,
They make you feel dead.
They some how get deep,
way into your mind,
secrets they won't keep,
and more they will find.
They share them with friends,
so people can hear,
your rumour is out,
and so is your fear.
They ruin it all,
your life they could end,
too strong and too tall,
for you to defend.
They punch and they kick,
their words are so strong,
they are so sick,
they are so wrong.
They do have a lot,
and they are so smart,
But one thing they don't have,
is a good heart.

Lara Gelmetti (13)
Beechwood Sacred Heart School, Tunbridge Wells

Drugs

Why take drugs?
It's a whole lot of fuss,
It costs a lot of money,
And it's not even funny,
It makes you go mad,
And smell really bad,
Why waste your money?
Just spend it on something useful,
Why take drugs it's just a waste of time,
When you could be spending your money having a good time.

Samuel Taylor (13)
Beechwood Sacred Heart School, Tunbridge Wells

Toby Said

Toby said:
'Mum.'
'Dad.'
'Dog, boo!'
'Yes!'
'No!'

Toby Baldwin Charles (12)
Chailey Heritage School, North Chailey

In The Garden

Mum saw me singing in the garden.
Dad and Freddie the dog were exercising in the garden too.
That made me happy.
We all ended up singing and dancing in the garden.

Henry Schofield (13)
Chailey Heritage School, North Chailey

When I Was A Baby

When I was a baby
I loved water,
Swimming,
Playing on the floor,
Learning to roll over,
My first pair of special Piedro boots,
Standing in my stander having fun!

Francesca Powell (13)
Chailey Heritage School, North Chailey

My Teaching Assistants

My teaching assistants are happy and good.
They make me cheerful,
When we do drama, dance and singing,
My teaching assistants make me laugh.
Together we have fun and laugh.
That is what makes school fun,
Happy, good, cheerful and a laugh.

Nina Potter (16)
Chailey Heritage School, North Chailey

Princess In A Caravan

I know a princess,
Her name is Sophie.
She is lazy
And lives in a caravan in Chichester!
She has two sisters called Liz and Sherrie.
Princess Sophie is young, smooth and messy!

Jade Stapleton (13)
Chailey Heritage School, North Chailey

Bodies Of Sin

All we are is bitter
Inside we are all dying,
Nothing but broken dreams and litter
But outside we're not even crying.

Can't understand why
We are all hurt
And why everyone we love seems to die
Our lovers nothing but bodies in the dirt

Cannot stand to be apart
All our demons come from within,
Can't live with a broken heart
In our heads, there's nothing but sin.

Megan Barnet (15)
Chamberlayne College, Weston

Leopard

One slick tail,
One silk-covered body,
Two marble eyes,
Spying, prancing, dancing
Like a stealthy plane,
The secret assassin of the Congo.

Ben Donohoe (12)
Charters Ancaster School, Bexhill-On-Sea

Seasons

Seasons, seasons they can change how we act,
They change the weather on a yearly schedule
And that's an honest fact.

Some people were classed a fool
Because they thought it was witchcraft and other magic,
But it was actually the seasons
Now that's an honest fact.

Adam Wates (11)
Coopers Technology College, Chislehurst

Recipe For A Good Meal

A good meal,
The best recipe it requires,
To fill your mouth with flavour,
And lovely goodness.

Contents of a best recipe;
Well the food mixes,
Excellent presentation have it must,
Amazingly planned it must please.

Dishes from with world;
Spanish paella
French croquet monsieur,
Indian curry,
English fry up.
Flavourful bits every time,
My watery mouth becometh a waterfall,
Rumble, rumble,
My gargantuan stomach says,
More it wants, but cannot get.

Zack McGrath (11)
Coopers Technology College, Chislehurst

Mangos

I love this exotic fruit,
Whilst they are tucked away,
Somewhere secret,
I like to munch on these all day and night,
My mum is hiding the mangos,
Where are they hiding?
I like young ones,
Middle aged ones as well,
I really like big ones,
They are what I crave.
I buy them in Tesco, ASDA, Sainsbury's,
I always love them maybe.
I love mangos more than chocolate,
The sweet taste is so divine,
It makes my mouth water more than ever.

Charlie Wait (11)
Coopers Technology College, Chislehurst

Never . . .

Two eyes that never saw,
A button nose that never received sweet aromas,
One mouth where taste buds never developed,
Two ears never pricked up to hear,
Ten fingers never feeling,
Two hands never held tight,
Ten toes never wriggled with excitement,
One tummy never tickled by another,
A head of hair never combed,
One voice never sang a tune.

You never took a breath, but you continuously take my breath away,
You're up there while I'm down here,
Hopefully sometime it will be the day –
For us to meet, but only if you may?

Chloe King (12)
Coopers Technology College, Chislehurst

High And Low

Indulged by the warmth of their house,
Denied by the warmth of day, threatened by the cold of night.
Loved by the city,
Despised by the people.

Pose! Pose! Let the camera go wild,
Please! Please! I beseech you
Not a drop of sweat falls from the pure being,
But a waterfall from the tainted human.

Attracted by the heat of nature,
The glory of fame beckons.
Love burnt through the blazing object of heat,
Respected by the town.

Now his life's a misery, pursued by the wolves of the day.
Visited by the doves of kismet; changed his life perpetually.

Princess Terin Ighedosa (12)
Coopers Technology College, Chislehurst

Spring

Spring is like spring,
Blooming and bouncing,
Pushed down and away,
But brought back soon enough,
It leaves me and you,
But always comes back,
All bouncing and blooming.

Netra Shah (11)
Coopers Technology College, Chislehurst

Outside My Front Door

The infernos and blood spilt,
The lives on both sides, cruelly dealt,
The deaths of many just outside my front door,
This is the Great World War,
With all memories, so vividly recalled,
At the time, I felt so small,
But now I realise I must've stood tall,
To be alive and able to remember,
The deaths of so many, just outside my front door.
The armoured dragon's temple my home,
The pops of gun fire turn into a drone.
Friends dead, comrades laying prone,
Grown men sick with fear.
Long range gunmen fire from a cliff, so sheer,
The deaths of so many, just outside my front door,
Teammates losing limbs and lives,
For what?

Ned Tregidden (11)
Coopers Technology College, Chislehurst

Meow, I Want Food!

What can I do to make them give me food?
I could purr and roll over and go mew, mew!
Or I could go outside, act lonely and sad,
And then they'll feed me, then I'll be glad!

What do I do to get some jelly, meaty Whiskas?
Or some of them lovely, delicious crunchy biscuits
They really are nice, but what can I do,
To get,
My scrumptious,
Delectable,
Food?

Sarah Jane Waddington (11)
Coopers Technology College, Chislehurst

Love

Love;
The way your heart beats
When you see their face,
You would kill someone with a mace
For them,
Love;
The only thing that isn't boring,
The thing that gets you up in the morning,
The person you want to be calling,
Is your one and only
Love;
Nerves in your tummy,
You know that she is yummy,
She is really funny,
I guess that's love?
Love;
You stay up all night,
But you are still ready to fight
For your one and only,
Love;
You went to hers for dinner,
When you got asked you felt like a winner,
One day she will be yours . . .
She will be yours forever
Well I guess that is just love . . .

Alexander Henbest (11)
Coopers Technology College, Chislehurst

YOLO

Y ou never should stop,
O nly stopping to tell people to,
L ive life to the full,
O nce life stops it's like it never begun.

Brogan Fearne (12)
Coopers Technology College, Chislehurst

Summer

S is for summer, that's what this poem's about,
U is for unbeatable, that's what summer is,
M is for Mum and that's who I'll be nagging a lot,
M is also for me, that's who will be getting a tan,
E is for energy, what I won't have a lot of,
R is for relaxing, that's what I love!

Jacob Tull (12)
Coopers Technology College, Chislehurst

Rugby

Running, tackling and falling to the ground,
That's what rugby can be about,
People get hurt when they hit their head,
When they bleed their outfit goes red,

They are always running about,
When they get angry they often shout,
Players are strong and rugby is great,
Ultimate players get no rate,

The thing I like most is that they destroy everything in their path,
And when they win a massive game, they have a celebratory bath,
I love watching England, they play so well,
And when we beat New Zealand, well that's a story to tell,

When teams run up the staircase,
It's like getting to last base,
The team has won the trophy,
They all celebrate so brilliantly.

David Sutherland (12)
Coopers Technology College, Chislehurst

Food

Eating, eating, eating,
The delight of glorious food
It's a lot better than getting a beating,
It gets me in a good mood.

Some foods I absolutely hate
Like couscous or tomatoes,
It makes me say, 'Wowcher,'
However, I like potatoes.

Creamy chocolate
Saucy spaghetti
This all tastes very nice,
Especially with some spice.

Food is wonderful
What do you like? Chocolate, sweets?
Do you agree, food makes you feel wonderful?

Although today, there are lots of foods
I will stick to what I like.
I feel very strong about food.

What about meals
The best one is spaghetti Bolognese
I bet you like it? Don't you!

So that's what it's all about;
Glorious food,
After reading this, I hope you're in a good mood.

Freddy Flaherty (11)
Coopers Technology College, Chislehurst

Summer

S unny and cheerful, the children play.
U p and down the hills, they play all day.
M ost of the children jump and splash in the pool.
M any of the children don't like being splashed at all.
E very young person loves ice cream.
R unning around the playground, they all scream.

Steven Belsham (12)
Coopers Technology College, Chislehurst

The Seasons

Snow falls in the park
Cold, dark, long nights are gloomy,
Christmas is coming.

Spring is here new life
Is coming to the world
As the sun rises.

Blue sky and ice cream
Always having some good fun,
Summer time is here.

These are the different seasons
That bring good and bad times,
These are the reasons for
Getting rid of the old and in with the new.
That is life for everyone.

Charlotte Dowling (11)
Coopers Technology College, Chislehurst

Emotion Poem

Red is for anger.
Black is for darkness.
Yellow is for happiness,
Pink is for love.
Green is for sadness.
Orange is for frustration.
White is for emptiness.

Kristopher Abbott (11)
Coopers Technology College, Chislehurst

Seasons

Summer, hot by day
Ice cream and twilight by night,
This is summer, nice.

Dead leaves at my feet,
Red, gold and brown crackling fire,
This is the autumn

Falling all around me, you
And the trees stand silent,
Snow so cold and white.

Squirrels and birds scattered all around,
The sun shines as bright as the night sky,
So hot it could burn you with happiness,
Spring.
Amazing.

Max Micklewhite (11)
Coopers Technology College, Chislehurst

Spring

As the sun began to stir,
The animals opened their eyes,
The wind rushed through their tired fur,
And you could hear their children's cries.

'We're hungry, we're hungry, we want to eat,'
Their parents told them to, 'Wait, wait, wait,
You are going to undertake a ghastly feat,
We're going to have to scavenge all through the week.'

They gathered many different things,
Like nuts and grapes,
There were many different noises like thumps and pings,
Then Dad cried, 'Squirrels we do hate!'

Mum guzzled grapes,
Dad nuzzled nuts,
All day long you would hear, 'Squirrels we do hate!
With all our bruises and cuts.'

Each animal wanders through the bush
Looking for its food,
All quiet and hush
Looking for its food.

Spring is the season we all love,
When many different birds come out,
Like the pigeon and the dove
I watch this happening from my house.

One day I wish that I could see,
These animals live in harmony.

Oliver James Girling (12)
Coopers Technology College, Chislehurst

Depths Of Hell

Have you travelled through the depths of Hell?
The smell of burning flesh, blood and guts.
The shouts of men calling, screaming.
The rat-a-tat-tat of machinery.
I travelled to the depths of Hell.
The depths of Hell were in Belgium 1916,
The Somme.
The mud filled with rats and limbs.
Men hanging on barbed wire.
Puddles chest deep, a red as rubies.
Smoke and fires all around.
The darkness is blinding.
The battlefield that is no-man's-land is black.
Artillery hit the ground before us, causing the ground to erupt.
From the distance I make out a clanging sound.
I do not see as the fog is so thick, so overwhelming,
Clang, clang.
I dart for my webbing,
Though I do not find what I'm looking for.
I got it just in time,
But one does not find what he's looking for.
He chokes, he stumbles, his eyes roll,
He is as sick as all this,
All this that is war.

Liam Sale-Sharp (12)
Coopers Technology College, Chislehurst

Death In Sandy Valley

Walking, walking, walking,
Further than the longest marathon,
Every step hurts, the feeling has gone,
And now it is time to give.

Slipping and sliding on the sand
Walking, walking, no one would think,
Of mist in the desert
Nothing in sight, not even a man.

A light, a light
I gaze upon a light,
Shining brighter than the sun
Suddenly, it appeared.

Begging me closer and closer
Until I can almost touch it,
Suddenly, everything feels better
Death has won and I have lost.

Left by my own kind
To die and rot,
In the desert
Left, alone, alone.

At once, I see beauty.
Jessica, made it to Heaven,
Now it's time for my test
Have I been good or bad?

Sent down and down until,
I can see the lights of Hell,
I have failed the test
I have eternity, here, alone.

Christopher MacNeil (12)
Coopers Technology College, Chislehurst

George Jardine

G eorge is my name
E xecutioner on the Xbox game
O ld grandad is my claim to fame
R eputation as a good footballer
G lad to be a Cray Wanderer
E xtreme scooting is my hobby

J ourneying to Gravesend with my cousin Bobby
A double whip, bar spin and manual test
R evolution skatepark is the best
D etermination, skills and then a well deserved rest
I have a sister called Bonnie
N aughty she is and a girlfriend of Ronnie
E nding our fights, I'll always say sorry.

George Jardine (11)
Coopers Technology College, Chislehurst

Freddie Walters

F reddie is the name
R unning is the game,
E ve is my sister,
D aring
D evil,
I ntelligent,
E nthusiastic.

W hining is what I do,
A ll day,
L earning,
T oday,
E very day, for the next five years,
R egretting what I've done,
S ince I was young.

Freddie Walters (12)
Coopers Technology College, Chislehurst

School

Add a tea spoon of teachers
And a sprinkle of kids
With a dash of lessons
And a pinch of determination
With a jar of rules.
Stir it until the lessons go up into flames,
Then put it in the microwave until the rocket explodes
And the kids come up in spats,
Put it on a plate and wait for five minutes,
What do you get?
A school of course.

Kieran Pemberton (12)
Coopers Technology College, Chislehurst

Knife Crime

The end of life will soon arrive
And all will be left is dust,
No light, no warmth, no love, no faith,
All dead was once alive.

No heart, no soul, no time, no life,
All will soon be gone,
Just weariness and questions I ask,
They cut me like a knife.

No family, no courage, no emotions I feel,
My mind stays awake,
But my body shuts down.
I grab my wound, my hand comes back red,
The blade still etched in my skin,
He did it for no reason, just out of the blue.

My body weak, my mind messed up,
But I'm still strong in thought,
At least I didn't let a knife cut my life short.

Madison Lyon (12)
Coopers Technology College, Chislehurst

Dog Delusion

I was walking one day in a meadow
When I saw something I didn't want to see.
There stood on all fours,
It was coming for me!

I turned and started for the trees
Staring to move faster, I tripped
And fell to the dirt, he was running straight in my direction,
But I couldn't move, I was hurt!
Yet still I was on high alert.

To my surprise it had caught me!
I cried for help, but nobody came,
The struggle took all my strength,
But I managed to get away!

I ran without a thought
I made sure I hadn't left a trail,
My chance of escape was short!
Like a banshee it let out a wail!

The creature was right behind me
Perhaps only a few feet!
So I turned and pulled it out of my pocket
And gave the dog its treat!

Charlie Baker (12)
Coopers Technology College, Chislehurst

Animal Equality!

Their eyes weep for the future,
But little do they know.
They would fall one by one,
And their future would be none.

Is it you who causes this?
Is it you who causes the pain?
Although they don't die in vain,
It could be you who makes them suffer.

They're your responsibility,
They are dependent on you.
While you leave them alone,
You don't hear their crying moan.

You leave them while they're close to death,
Until they're ready to fall.
You leave them there, on the wall,
Ready for the other side.

They're not safe until there is a call,
Rescued from their dark future.
Revenge is not a feature,
But prosecution is the law.

Seniz James (13)
Coopers Technology College, Chislehurst

Dandelion Boy

His hair, a small tuft of blond, his walk, different but proud,
Sitting in the meadow hours on end
Picking flowers and singing out loud.

At school adoration drowns him, they loved him to the end of the earth.
But as soon as he returned home,
He knew nothing of what he was worth.

Suddenly good things dropped, dread was posted through the door.
No one could even believe it,
The disgrace was up to war!

His satchel was packed at the ready, he was almost ready to leave,
His family gave him a formal farewell,
He told himself to believe.

He picked dandelions as he walked, shaking through pure fear,
He clutched them tightly as a good luck charm,
The soft boy shed not one tear.

The flowers were tight in his hand, arriving at camp soon after,
Soldiers laughed and giggled at his foolish attempt,
These words were heard through the laughter;

Dandelion boy, dandelion boy,
He's as soft as a willow tree,
Dandelion boy, dandelion boy,
He's as foolish as foolish can be.

He was given a shield and a sword, told it was a toy,
They encouraged him to use it,
Yet more slew by dandelion boy.

Once all were fighting, he appeared at the top of the hill,
One ferocious man sniggered.
He aimed his arrow to kill.
Dandelion boy, dandelion boy
With his art always at best,
Dandelion boy, dandelion boy
Who finally got shot in the chest.

Abbey Power (12)
Coopers Technology College, Chislehurst

Snow Falling Everywhere

S alt being scattered on the floor,
N aughty children throwing snowballs,
O ld people slipping and sliding everywhere
W indows covered in ice and snow.

F reezing cold snow everywhere,
A person slips over and everyone laughs
L ying in the snow and ice
L ots of snowmen being knocked down
I nside in the warm
N o sound at all
G usting wind outside howling life a wolf.

E verywhere snow
V ery slippery ice
E ven children slipping
R unning everywhere but slipping on the floor
Y et no one really cares if they fall over
W hite snow still falling
H appy children playing in the snow
E veryone is smiling left and right
R eally cold people, I can tell from their faces
E verywhere I can see, snow falling.

Max Pittom (12)
Coopers Technology College, Chislehurst

I Wish To Be . . .

A single tree, dead and cold,
I wish to be full of bloom.
A simple stream, frozen and stiff,
I wish to be, a trickle of shimmering waters
A world of white.
I wish to be, a meadow of gracious, green grass.
With dazzling dew drops, in the sun's light,
Swaying in the spring's breeze.

Carmel Simmonds (12)
Coopers Technology College, Chislehurst

Cruelty To Animals

Cruelty to animals is wrong,
This poem might be a little long.
So just listen in,
Cruelty to animals is a sin.
Don't abandon them,
Near the River Thames.

Don't go fishing,
You will be wishing
Because it's cruel,
Even though dogs might drool.
It doesn't matter,
Just don't eat fish in batter.
Because it's cruel!

Be careful of cats,
Don't use animals for your hats.
Don't kill animals for their skins,
Don't put animals in bins,
Because it's cruel!

Don't kill animals for food
Just because it tastes nice, dude.
Don't take their lives,
While using knives.
Because it's cruel!
Pick them up off the street,
Before the sleet.
Don't forget it,
You will regret it.
Because it's cruel.

Phoebe Grove (12)
Coopers Technology College, Chislehurst

Nightmares

I breathe, I live, I hope, I die and yet I do not dream,
When the stars fall from the Heavens,
And God's breath caresses my face,
Those hellish, hellish cries,
Those hellish, hellish thoughts,
Possess my head.

Sweat trickles down my back,
I jump and twitch in fright,
When I open my eyes,
Darkness swallows my view,
And I think, *why do I deserve this?*

The moon is the nightguard,
The stars are like the lights,
The owl is like the officer,
The room is the prison,
My bed is the torturer.

I look up to God,
To the angels,
To the devil,
And I ask myself,
Why am I here?

Zainab Khan (13)
Coopers Technology College, Chislehurst

Doom

Doom has overcome me,
It stays around my soul,
It kills my last hope,
And defeats me into death.

Doom has been my enemy,
It never goes away,
My whole mind is empty,
As I lie dead in the field.

Doom has stolen all,
From everyone, everywhere.
You cannot run, you cannot hide,
But is this really fair?

Thomas Butcher (12)
Coopers Technology College, Chislehurst

The End Of Me . . .

Life goes on, as they always say
I always thought so, until this very day
Hide or run, none will work
Because inside of me, evil will always lurk.

It isn't fair how this must end,
It's driving my brain around the bend
I want it to stop, the worry and the pain
This is ten times worse than the remorseless cane.

No family or friends,
Impossible to make amends.
As hard as I may try,
At the end of this, I will surely die.

I am all alone, no such thing as fun
Thank goodness for the quick shot of a gun
Slowly count, 1 . . . 2 . . . 3
This will be the end of me.

Toni Johns (13)
Coopers Technology College, Chislehurst

Death

Death can be a thief. Stealing people when it's not their time,
When they have done nothing wrong. Not one single crime.
Although he could be a saviour,
Stopping people's pain.
When disease has spread, or if they might die in vain.
Families weep and mourn, for their loved one or friend,
When death sounds the horn.
He will come for anyone, no one knows why,
Why the coin has chosen you to die.
Who knows what death is like?
Is he a skeletal figure? Does he hold a spike?
Do you close your eyes and see a light
When your body has lost the will to fight?
Do you get a judgement for Heaven or Hell?
A chance to redeem yourself before the hammer has fell.
Will he take you during the dead of night?
The man in the hooded cloak full of terrifying might.
Or will you be taken during midday,
No matter what month, June or May?
He comes so quickly before you can see,
Your family to say goodbye, now you pay the fee.
He will carry you to the horizon, edge of the world
There, right before your eyes, your destiny unfurled.
When it comes to death, no one can win,
Especially if you deserve it, for committing a sin.
He comes before, you can be scared,
When it comes to death, no one is prepared.

Georgina Carpenter
Coopers Technology College, Chislehurst

Feel Like A Fool

As you hurt the innocent boy in the corner.
His face full of sadness and despair.
What has this world come to?
All the wrongs these people do.
You decide the path of evil.
But inside what are you hiding?
You kick, you punch, you call him names, without even minding.
Are you doing this because you're insecure, you have no friends,
Or simply you wanna be the big man?
But when you next go to hurt someone,
Don't act cool,
Think of the defenceless boy you make feel like a fool.

Katie Beaton (13)
Coopers Technology College, Chislehurst

Are Witches Really Mean?

Witches are ugly, creepy and mean,
But are all princesses a perfect sunbeam?
They get what they want not an hour of work paid,
They sit on their bum, not a finger is laid.
Witches have broomsticks, but a princess has slaves,
They don't rent out houses, but rent out damp caves.
They have long noses and a tall pointy hat
And some of them may have a black and white cat.
They walk all night and cackle all day,
But princesses always get their own way.
Princesses are lazy and act like a machine,
So tell me now, is that witch really mean?

Shannon Bethany Pemberton (12)
Coopers Technology College, Chislehurst

Untitled

A wandering moon glitters
Brightly in the jet black night,
Stars surround the beautiful sight,
Each one of those beautiful burning lights
Has a lot of majestic might,
Eyes that shine and wander high
Look up the glittering sky.
They blink, they twitch and shut in tight
To make that loving wish on this very special night.

Liberty-Rose Lyttle (11)
Coopers Technology College, Chislehurst

Light

As I woke on this summer's day . . .
The shine that met my dull sleepy eyes.
A great complexion of heat and wind blowing through my curtains.
Overloaded happiness bursting out,
The great feelings of fantastic dilemmas.
Warm recurring breeze bouncing on my face.
Flamboyant whistling of bright birds,
Laughter ringing from the joyful children playing.
As I lick the dripping vanilla ice cream,
How I wonder how thee keeps a dark world alight,
One more precious than the most valuable of metals I can't believe,
Light . . .
Light . . .
Light . . .

Raheem Olaniyonu (12)
Coopers Technology College, Chislehurst

Peace Is Made By All

Peace can be made by many young and old,
But too many people die a day,
So to make this right we all have to fight,
What the world has in store for all.

Think about the famine and diseases
Which people suffer from each day,
The people with the guns in their hands,
Are the guilty ones.

Let's all come together as a country
Feeling ready and brave
All prepared for what we may discover
In this world today.

Tia Roberts (12)
Coopers Technology College, Chislehurst

I'll Always Be There

All through the year,
Happiness is near,
Throughout all the seasons,
Whether there's beacons,
Or even snow,
You know where you can go.

It may be cold,
Or the fall,
You may loathe,
But you know who you can call,
When you feel down,
I'll be there.

The January blues,
Might get you,
But look for the fun,
Playing in the sun,
Your heart was a flame,
It wasn't to blame.

Grace Tompsett (11)
Coopers Technology College, Chislehurst

Ziggy Stardust

Z ooming around the park,
I lluminated white fur,
G ood . . . sometimes,
G rins when he's hyper running around the house,
Y oung little legs that jump over the heather,

S mall dog but big inside
T ail as he wags it when there is another dog in sight,
A nyone would stop to stroke his soft fur,
R ed tongue as he licks his lips for food,
D igs as he buries his toy and treat in the garden,
U rge to run when he spots something he likes,
S cottish Highlands where he comes from
T rouble he causes taking things that are not his,

Ziggy Stardust might seem naughty, but he's a dog!

Cara Netherton (11)
Coopers Technology College, Chislehurst

Pring

The long cold winter is melting away,
A single red bird was spotted today.

Through the mist the sun is peeking,
Squirrels are about and acorn-seeking.

New life has come to the fields and woods,
Kids venture out with sweatshirts and hoods.

In just a few weeks the river will flow,
Blossoms on the trees will start to show.

There's still a chill in the springtime air,
Winter is gone but the memory is still there.

Summer is waiting a few months beyond,
To warm the air, the meadow and the pond.

A gopher peers out from the holes that he makes,
Springtime is when the whole word wakes.

Kiera Withers (11)
Coopers Technology College, Chislehurst

Ever After

Approaching the home,
Although it wasn't her own
Unlocking the door . . .
Click, click, click
She entered without fear.

Explored, and it was clear,
She gave every room a check,
Even sleeping in each bed.

As they arrived
Home at last,
The bed she slept in,
Covered in blood,
The motionless pain
Gave no sound.

The end was near,
Goldilocks was bound.

No more tales of fun and laughter,
The end is near, forever after.

Katie Edge (13)
Coopers Technology College, Chislehurst

Be Yourself

It's such a waste of time
Being someone that you're not,
You're mirroring a mime
And I think it's time you stop!

It may take courage
But it'll be worth it,
It's weighing you down,
And you look like a clown.

It may seem different
Not trying to fit in,
Your fight for acknowledgement,
Must feel like a sin.

Stepping on friends for social standing?
Will it make you popular?
Or are you crash landing?

Try being just you
Maybe for a day,
You don't have a clue
What it takes to be you.

We may not look or feel the same
We all like different things,
But one thing we have in common,
We are all human beings!

Georgie Weller (14)
Crofton School, Stubbington

Winter Day

Snow is really cold,
It can freeze you to the heart.
Winter's a season,
A season of thick warm clothes.
People stay in homes and sleep.

Deer playing in snow,
Fur as brown as chocolate.
Snow-covered branches.
Their bushy tails wagging.
Icy white spots on bodies.

Children laugh and play,
As they build giant snowmen.
Adults stay indoors,
Drinking their hot chocolate.
All the fingers are freezing.

Shae Parker (11)
Folkestone School for Girls, Folkestone

Society

S omeone who's there for you,
O pposite on the street,
C ommunity,
I n your neighbourhood,
E ver near you,
T rustworthy and reliable,
Y outh and adults.

Lauren Little (12)
Folkestone School for Girls, Folkestone

The Clouds Are Crying

The clouds are crying,
They are very sad,
They let their tears fall,
Onto the Earth below,
Everyone's happy,
Because of the rain.

But one little girl,
Is also sad,
She feels the clouds pain,
Because of death,
Her grandma has died,
Who was close to her.

As she stares out the window,
At the rainy day outside.
She remembers the fun times,

She stays strong,
And does not cry.
She puts on her coat,
And goes outside.

She looks up at the clouds.
Letting the rain drip on her face.
The clouds stop crying,
And let out the sun.
Because little girl was strong,
And so where they.

Emily Chard (12)
Folkestone School for Girls, Folkestone

Springtime

New life all around,
The green grass that surrounds.
Trees growing blossom everywhere,
Running around are the newborn hares.

Sun getting warm,
As the farm animals are born.
Children eating Easter eggs,
Bunnies hopping by their legs.
Tulips and daffodils begin to bloom,
Everyone saying goodbye to the gloom.

Spring is here,
Everyone cheer.
Bring on the Easter parade,
Everyone drinking homemade lemonade!

Megan Davis (12)
Folkestone School for Girls, Folkestone

Rain, I See

Rain, I see through my eyes,
The sun disappears from the sky and dies.
I do not like a rainy day,
The road is wet, the sky is grey.
The torrent forced them to stay to their height,
Composure swayed by onerous might.
It spits and pours like mighty claws,
We all look and run towards shelters and doors.
Flooded puddles almost like a pool,
The sky laughs at us as if we were fools.
Stamp-stamp, splish-splash, wellies come flying from the air,
Drip-drop, drop-drop, water slips from our hair.
The sun says, 'Hello again!' Now we're all dry,
So now it's time to say goodbye!

Suhana Miah (12)
Folkestone School for Girls, Folkestone

Equal Rights

Every day I say to myself,
Will there be peace?
Will there be friendship?
Can the bridges ever be repaired?
Or will we always be wondering, 'What if?'

Every day I say to myself,
Can we not make amends?
Is humanity so depraved that it will,
For evermore divide citizens,
And drive them to despair?

Every day I say to myself,
Will it – not ever – allow us to unite?
To make us feel like we belong.
All the hate, pain, endurance
Driven to the end of their wits.

Every day I think to myself,
If ever we needed something,
It would be this,
To unite amongst ourselves and,
Regardless of colour, sex, religion,
Love one another the way we are destined to.

Now I say; they,
We can do it –
And we will –
To make this world a better place,
For you and for me.

Visaka Gurung (12)
Folkestone School for Girls, Folkestone

Who Are We?

Who are you, you ask?
Why don't you guess,
By the end of the story,
I'll surely confess.

You'll see us on Facebook,
We may even tweet you.
We'll catch you on Instagram,
Or BBM too.

We will be downloading music
Or playing on iPhones.
Collecting apps,
In a couple of taps.

We are noisy and loud,
We use slang all around.
'BTW, FYI, OMG'
Who are we?

Can you guess who we are yet?
Or should I tell you the answer?
All together let's say,
We are the youth of the day!

Rachel Stredwick (12)
Folkestone School for Girls, Folkestone

War, What Is Good For?

Marching proudly into the battle,
When all of a sudden the ground rattles,

In the middle, where do I go?
But when I see a blinding glow.

It comes no faster than any bullet,
As I clutch my good luck bracelet,

The blow, however, never touches me,
But flies right past and strikes my enemy.

A bleeding head he has before him,
As well as a slice right down his aching limb.

I touch his heart as his eyes slowly close,
Then cover his body in my clothes.

Sitting up straight, I gaze around,
Staring at all the helpless mounds.

I knew then that this wouldn't be easy,
But at that I felt uneasy.

War doesn't care who it kills,
As long as, in the end, everything is still.

Erin Lambert (12)
Folkestone School for Girls, Folkestone

So Many Questions . . .

As I wildly whip past, I see the glorious ice caps fall to their death,
I see the sea levels rising and families rushing to save their lives –
Why does it happen? How can it stop?
So many questions,
None thought about a lot.
This is the ruins of a beautiful world –
It used to be a Mercedes of towering trees,
But now it's the Volvo of ugly stumps.
The air is as disgusting as the boys' toilets.
Incredibly evil poachers grab their guns,
Why does this happen? How can it stop?
So many questions,
None thought about a lot.
As the breath of the Earth, I see everything,
And everything that needs to stop.
I see innocent men being shot down,
What have they done to us?
Why does this happen? How can it stop?
So many questions,
None thought about a lot,
Until today.

Kazia Pyott (11)
Folkestone School for Girls, Folkestone

What Is Right And What Is Wrong?

What is right and what is wrong?
Why can't everyone just live in harmony?
Red and blue makes purple,
Blue and yellow makes green,
Black and white makes grey, but it seems to be that they don't matter.

What is right and what is wrong?
Fighting, shouting and abusing others because of their skins is not the way.
Smiling, laughing and getting along are right.
One man once had a dream.
A dream that two different colours would unite, so let's try, it's not hard.

What is right and what is wrong?
Racism means harm.
Going home and crying yourself to sleep.
We are all the same inside.
Nasty comments because of your skin.
None of it makes sense.
No one deserves to be treated badly.
Have a dream, think hard, mean something and fight for happiness.

Anna Philcox (12)
Folkestone School for Girls, Folkestone

For This Is What I Dream For

When is the time to be equal again?
The time to walk side by side
Not someone in front or behind,
But just a line of equality and hope.

For this is what I dream for
A world that allows differences
And embraces every difference each person has,
Shows them off as if it is a gold medal
And loves every part of them,
For this is what I dream for.

When will the world change
Its prejudices and thoughts
About people who are different?
Even though they are each beautiful and lovely
And all need to be loved.
For this is what I dream for.

Agna Chungbang (11)
Folkestone School for Girls, Folkestone

Why?

Why can't people get along and truly be a united nation?
Why can't we have peace and stamp out discrimination?
Why can't we realise that we are all special and important?
Why can't we stop it, stop being so ignorant?

We should be able to stand calmly together,
We should stand confident, and not be offensive to each other,
We should be happy, we should have joy,
We should be united, man and woman, girl and boy!

I pray for tomorrow to be better,
I pray for people to be accepted, whatever their colour,
I pray for discrimination to happen no longer,
So we can stand together – together even stronger!

Natasha Jaie Phillips (12)
Folkestone School for Girls, Folkestone

Nature

Nature is a part of our lives,
Natural things don't just come to us like chives,
Everything is natural, even ourselves,
But the things are not, as from our shelves.

It's not every day that it shines all day,
So enjoy the moment while you can today,
Sometimes it pours and makes us cry,
But the enjoyment comes from an apple pie.

The gentle sea sways, just like the waves,
But not like the mysterious branches, as they behave,
It effortlessly turns into a beautiful blossom tree,
Just like, the beautiful blue Coral Sea.

The summer springs, as if it's a spring,
The shadow hangs on like as if it's engagement,
A summer's picnic day is just perfect for a party,
With the joy and laughter from all is a good old smarty,
Looking for a wonderful day out every day.

Pragati Thapa (11)
Folkestone School for Girls, Folkestone

Willow Trees

W stands for willow trees
I solated all alone
L ooking for some happiness
L ooking for some love
O bserving all the people
W alking with their loved ones

T rying to fill the emptiness
R eaching out for companionship
E nvy taking over all emotion
E choing loud and clear that I am simply . . .
S itting in silent solitude!

Sophie Fawcett-Jones (11)
Folkestone School for Girls, Folkestone

Pollution

This morning I was walking to school,
I could hear grown-ups shouting, 'Pollution, pollution.'
I didn't know what it was so I just ignored,
And walked past them.

I could smell gas or something burning,
So I ran until the school having pollution in my head,
The school was closed and quit,
I got scared and ran even more.

My heart's beating like horse's hoofs on a dirt road,
What a strange feeling.
I started crying and slowly I collapsed.
My hands started shaking and I shouted, 'Help.'
No one could hear me so I cried even more.

Next minute I woke up and found myself with my nan
I thought she was dead
I could see God and a land of angels,
Where am I?
I questioned myself, I must be in Heaven,
The place where dreams come true!

Vanessza Borbas (12)
Folkestone School for Girls, Folkestone

Youth Of Today

Youth
Rookie, embryonic
Imaginative, creative, adapting,
A diverse standard of people
Juvenile.

Jennifer Chhantyal (12)
Folkestone School for Girls, Folkestone

The Seasons

Spring is here,
As picturesque flowers begin to blossom,
The serene atmosphere approaches,
Animals are brought into the world,
They graze with joy upon the hilltops,
Full of freedom they wander endlessly.
A time of new life is spring,
Summer is here,
The sun floats on the horizon elegantly,
Scorching summer days,
Delicious, mouth-watering, and luxurious, the smell of barbecues,
Wafting around, it creates a tempting aroma.
A beaming sun glaring at the world,
Waves caressing against a golden shore,
Rugged rocks surrounding the sun-kissed beach.
Autumn is here.
Naked trees stripped of their leaves,
Their imposing, skeleton-like fingers claim victim after victim,
A veil of mist in the sky,
Cold bitter weathers are near,
Spine-chilling whistling wind,
Winter is here,
Idyllic snowflakes fill the air,
A blanket of snow covers the ground,
The festive seasons,
Joy, hope and family.

Amelia Burton (11)
Folkestone School for Girls, Folkestone

My Rights, Your Rights, Our Rights

To express yourself happily,
Without being discriminated
Is how the world should be.
People get bullied because of disability,
But we are all the same you and me.

We all believe in different religions
Because we all have
To make the decisions.
Some get bullied because of their gender,
But to be perfectly fair,
It does not really matter.

Whether you are black or white,
At the end of the day
We all have a right.
We all have a right,
To live free
And not in abuse or slavery.

Nyasha Sakuringwa (12)
Folkestone School for Girls, Folkestone

Current Affairs

What if we had no wars?
Children wouldn't be affected, evacuated and homeless.
No food to eat clean water to drink.
What if we had no wars?
Half way across the country, guns would be shot.
Screaming in pain,
Blood splattered all over the place, imagine living in a war zone,
Danger creeps around every corner,
You scream and scream in agony until there's total silence.
What if we had no wars?
Little children wouldn't wander around the streets,
Calling for their parents until they realise they're not coming back.
How long do you think they would survive out there in the war zone?
What if we had no wars?
The world would come to a final peace
Children united with their families, no need for starvation and dirty water.
But instead we want them to be happy, healthy and hopeful,
But that's just my dream.

Sonia Gurung (12)
Folkestone School for Girls, Folkestone

Why?

Emily Davidson who died while trying
Tried to throw a banner over the King's horse
At the Epsom Derby on June 5th 1913,
But sadly got hit on the course.

Why did this happen?
Why did she have to throw a banner?
She got completely flattened
She didn't do this for glamour.

This was caused by something horrible
Which will hopefully never happen again,
They will always be historical,
The suffragettes were their names.

They suffered from working all day
While men had the rights to sit around,
They were forced to stay
If they could, they would turn around.

The suffragettes are a good example
Of something we shouldn't have to mention,
Equal rights, are one of those,
Which you have to say, why?

Melissa Bentley (11)
Folkestone School for Girls, Folkestone

Equal Rights

Equal rights are only fair
For all woman if they dare,
To try to follow a career
Without pressure and any fear.

From teaching a class
To flying a plane,
From being a mechanic
Or driving a train.

A woman can do anything
That a man can do,
It's always been the case
And it's certainly still true.

From being in the police force
To riding a racehorse
Equal rights are only fair
For men and woman who really care.

Ella Nixon (11)
Folkestone School for Girls, Folkestone

Our Funny Government

John Major, he was the 'grey' man
Not fifty shades – more his suits,
Although during a chapter he didn't give two hoots.

Maggie Thatcher – no one can match her
Now Blair, which was he?
The one with the teeth? Or was that Ted Heath?
These are times of austerity, until we can return to prosperity.

The politicians sit on the benches
Fiddling their expenses,
Preaching family values
Always appearing on the news.

Oh Mr Speaker
Could things look any bleaker?
With this coalition
There is no vision!

Well hey presto!
I give you my manifesto,
Instead of votes, let's do it this way
Just how we do it on eBay

Bid for an idea,
Then see it appear
Just because we are too young doesn't mean we don't have a choice,
It's our country too and we have a voice.

Emma Godfrey (12)
Folkestone School for Girls, Folkestone

The World Around You . . .

I asked my teacher, what is global warming?
And then he replied with an official warning.
I could explain in many, many ways,
But a poem seems best to get out this maze.

Global warming is happening and we can stop this thing,
By preventing green house gases and doing recycling.
Look around at all the pollution,
Is it necessary and do we need a solution?

We should walk more, drive less,
Take note and try our best.
Buy more local produce not from afar,
So you wouldn't have to jump into the car.

Why wasn't the world like this 50 years ago,
Is it technology or have people just let go?
We only live on one planet but sometimes it seems more,
So what will you do for the environment? Will you open a door?

We need to get people more aware,
Of the harm they are doing even if it's just not fair.
We should live our lives in peace and harmony,
But what about the whole economy?

Can you figure out what you need to do,
Or do you need some inspiration before you go and choose?
Just recycle, switch off, walk more and more,
And you will become better than before.

Chloe Beardsley (11)
Folkestone School for Girls, Folkestone

An Underwater World

If the world got warmer,
The sea levels will rise,
Ice caps melting all the time,
Low-lying islands
Like giant swimming pools,
Drowning all the unadapted fools.

If the world got warmer,
Fish will thrive,
Their underwater world,
Taking over our dry lives,
We would all have to learn to swim to survive.

If the world got warmer,
Would we turn into fish?
Or would we still eat them from our dinner dish?
How would we survive?
Would we live on rocks,
Or would we take a deep dive?

If the world got warmer,
What would we do?
We'd live in an underwater world,
As happy as you.

Melissa Hill (12)
Folkestone School for Girls, Folkestone

Natural World

Rain is falling down my window pane,
But we are hiding in a safer place.
The rain is pattering along the pavement,
Rain, rain, falling on the street.

The sun is shining through my window,
It's breaking through the thunder clouds,
We can see the light peaking through,
And the rain stops too.

Snow is falling heavily down from the pale sky
Forming a white blanket on the cold hard concrete,
We make a snowman wearing a scarf and hat,
Making snow angels in the blanket.

A rainbow is glowing across the sky,
I see its colours,
They make my eyes light up,
As their colours shine bright.

Rheanna Chopping (11)
Folkestone School for Girls, Folkestone

I Remember You

I wrote your name in the stars, it was all a dream.
I saw a ghost of you passing by, tears fell down my cheeks.
Remembering the times we had together, and the times you said you loved me
And the time we used to sit down and talk for hours by the sand.
I wish you were here to tell me one more time that you love me.

Lucy Kneeshaw (16)
Harbour Specialist School, Dover

Untitled

I'm twelve and my name is Katie.
Some people think I'm mad, other people hate me.
Don't get me wrong I do come across crazy.
Who are you to judge me, who are you to rate me.
Like I said before my name's Katie.
And I'm only twelve years old.
And I've got stories that should never be told.
Way back before the age of four years old.
And that's the stuff that made me be so bold.
I'm writing this today to show my real colour.
The things I've been through there is no other.
Some people try to find the real me, but I put up a cover.
To hide the emotional scars and stop the stutter.
This ain't fake, this is all real.
The stuff I've been that's why I can't chill.
Like a soldier doing another drill.
So like I said this is my story.
In all its blaze in all its glory.
Right now I feel like I'm on the highest storey.
Shouting out no fear, nothing for me.
So right here I shout out my name is Katie.

Katie Stevens (13)
Harbour Specialist School, Dover

Ode To The Night Sky

I grant I never saw the ancient fables unfurling.
Oh, great sails of the December twilight,
The Heaven-vaulted ceiling's
Thread pulls and draws my sight.
Perennially scrawled stories all revealing.

To the wonders above – those celestially peerless,
All faux glitz and ill purpose of below fades away.
Sky thickening with early morning's dew, disperses.
Even-tide's unholy cast comes out to play.

Atoms below yet ignorant,
Cassiopeia and her jealous children,
In dim moonlight, dance.
The plunge of nightfall.
Immortals' nonchalance.

Morpheus in-cape devours,
What light remains, diminished.
Sleepy sand caresses sleepy eyes,
All abed are dreaming, dream-shaping has finished.

But the pieces of sky are falling.
Canis and Ursa still yet starving.
Orion forever chasing the harsh mistress moon.
And all the while immortality grows jealous,
Yearning for our mortal sleep.

The ochre sky did gradate in the long hours that passed.
We lay underneath the stars –
The echoes of our past,
Telling tales of stories in the midnight sky.

And in our hearts,
Drawing out our own constellations.

Jack Mannings (17)
Havant Sixth Form College, Havant

War

Bang, bang, bang,
The guns fired,
As people dropped to the ground in pain,
Bombs dropped and as they did . . .
Bang!
Lives were lost,
Homes blown up,
Families broken,
And on it goes,
Never to stop,
Everyday they are remembered
By families of distraught,
Remembered by poppies, pictures and memories through all of love and life.

Karis Hesmer (12)
Helenswood Lower School, St Leonards On Sea

My Best Friend

My best friend, she is the best.
My best friend, she never rests.
My best friend, we have our problems.
My best friend, we always fight.
My best friend, I hate her now.
My best friend, she moved away.
My best friend, I miss her now.
My best friend, she moved back.
My best friend, she is the best.

Sophie Benton (12)
Helenswood Lower School, St Leonards On Sea

Guess The Pet

Pets can be cute and pets can be ugly.
They can be rough and they can be fluffy.
The pet that I want though, most of all,
Is one that will run around and chase a football.
Can you guess what this pet is?
It also likes to lick clean its dish.
They run around the garden after cats,
But some just like to sit and relax.
This pet is as cool as icicles,
It's even cooler than a bicycle?
So if you think you know the answer,
Flip over the paper and see if you're a master!

Catherine Brett (12)
Helenswood Lower School, St Leonards On Sea

Life! Live It! Love It!

Life, people say you only live once,
Some people only live for months,
Everyone has a life,
Even if it's only short.

At Every opportunity you get,
Grab it with both hands,
Never, never let it go,
Life, people say you only live once.

Live a life, live it eternally.

Mollie Worth (11)
Helenswood Lower School, St Leonards On Sea

Car Booty

As we walk out of the bushes,
And look at the stash,
We find our right places,
Now let's start dealing cash!

As we come to the stall,
And start talking money,
My grandad and I,
We are ever so cunning!

We'll beg and we'll bargain,
If we like it we must,
We'll make them go lower,
Until their prices go bust!

And when we go home,
My nanny will say,
'Where will we put it?
We can't put it away!'

As we walk out of the bushes,
And look to the stash,
We find our right places,
Now let's start dealing cash!

Eleanor Holman (12)
Helenswood Lower School, St Leonards On Sea

Giraffe, Giraffe

Giraffe, giraffe standing by
With a look of fear in his eyes,
Sees his enemy far away
Sees him eyeing up his prey.

Giraffe, giraffe innocent creature
His markings a magnificent feature,
Elegant like a ballroom dance
Turns his head for a single glance.

Giraffe, giraffe the time is near
Specifically when is still unclear,
Your predator is an experienced devil
His earlier victim alone and dishevelled.

Giraffe, giraffe such a shame
Without you it won't be the same.
You weren't quite quick enough this time
You were his prey, his organised crime.

Chantal Markowski (13)
Helenswood Lower School, St Leonards On Sea

Is War The End?

I stare down at the ground,
As my heart begins to race and pound,
I look at the metal killer in my hand,
Not strong, not brave but a coward I stand.

Ready to fight, ready to slaughter,
I can only hope and pray that I'll live to meet my new born daughter,
And I hope she won't grow up in a world such as mine,
Where each day it seems to rain even though I can see the sun shine.

Now I listen to the once calm air,
Turn to chaos as gun shots are fired everywhere,
I hear the cries as in agony they fall,
If only somebody could stop all this, anyone at all?

And maybe one day somebody will and war will end,
And all those broken hearts caused by it will be free to mend,
Yes I believe the future will be bright,
Because war will be out of mind and out of sight.

April Stansfield (12)
Helenswood Lower School, St Leonards On Sea

I Love You More Than Before

There's nothing we can't face
No chances we can't take,
Cause we're back together
And were stronger than ever.
I've got a lot to lose,
Until you're back on the booze
And if you don't
I'll keep hoping you won't,
Cause I love you more than I did before
And we will cope,
Just by having some hope,
Cause we love each other that bit more than before . . .

Collette Mitchell (12)
Helenswood Upper School, Hastings

Trench Feet

Blue like the sea, raw as ice,
Trench foot is not at all nice.
My feet are a minefield, *boom! Bang! Crash!*
My toes fall to the puddles, with a silent splash.

Pain crawls through my feet, the wind whipping me,
As I sit here glum, and so unhappy.
I miss my kids, I miss my wife,
I just want it return, to conventional life.

I perch in the dank, murky ditch,
As we prepare for battle, I begin to twitch.
The war bugles cry and the horses neigh,
The conflicts is now underway.

You sit at home as the days go by,
Glad not to be where soldiers lie.
You draw your blinds and stay discreet,
From the hellish place, where you get trench feet.

Natalie Andrews (13)
Helenswood Upper School, Hastings

Friends

A shoulder to cry on, when I'm in doubt,
My friends are people, whom I can't live without,
They console me and encourage me, but they inspire me more
My friends are the friends everyone looks for.

A friendship like ours obtains no flaws
There are no hidden agendas; we're true to our cores,
We're there for each other through thick and through thin
A friend is not bought, but earned from within.

Toni Doyle (13)
Helenswood Upper School, Hastings

Autumn

Autumn is the time of year,
When everybody comes here,
To the woods,
Everybody brings their goods!

When the trees have no leaves,
Everybody really believes
That autumn is magic,
And not at all tragic.

Maisie Mewburn (13)
Helenswood Upper School, Hastings

What I Feel Strongly About

Exmoor ponies on the moors,
Don't just sit around doing chores.
Their mane so bright,
It flows around like a kite.

They gallop up and down the moor,
People don't notice them like they don't notice the floor.
Please save Exmoor ponies,
All the myths and legends about them aren't phonies.

Their eyes glow silver in the sun,
And in the snow they all have fun.
Exmoor ponies are very clever,
Let's save them together.

Keep them alive today,
At Moorlandmousie.co.uk.
They gallop along the moor,
That's what I feel strongly for.

Hayley Eastabrook (12)
Helenswood Upper School, Hastings

Wonders Of Earth

The wonders of the Earth are hard to find,
so you should think inside your mind.
Mountain, waterfalls, lots of scenery –
Some of the things you will find extraordinary.

Birds, flowers, trees and skies
You can see above your eyes.
So many wonders we have in this industry,
heaven forbid that it
becomes history.

Human beings living in rapture,
thank goodness for Mother Nature.
Snow leopards, penguins and polar bears
living in their mothers' care.
Newborn babies crying for nourishment,
plants growing, soon they will flourish.

Cultures, nations, so many passions,
remember the war when we had to ration.
Towns and cities make up a country,
lots of people to keep you company.

If you search the Earth there will be wonders to see,
different places for you and for me.

Now you have found your place
In the world, don't take them for granted
Because they are the
Many wonders of Earth.

Tricia Kisakye (12)
Helenswood Upper School, Hastings

War

The soldiers fight a nasty battle.
We pray for safety among our cattle.
In the country on a farm.
Evacuees go, 'Excuse me ma'am.'

Our national anthem sung as we march,
Our lips go dry in the cold wind like starch.
We write letters home and are chilled to the bone,
It makes us want to groan and moan.
The battlefield is strewn with the dead.
We will go to Heaven if we die,
But to survive in a bed, life is hard for a soldier.
But once we have won we will be on a big fat boulder.

A saying goes a soldier gets the good in life:
A missus, a lovely girl of a wife.
Old London is bombed like mad.
Those evil Nazis are incredibly bad.
It hurts us to hear about those deaths,
But to see them is the worst just yet.
And if I were to make a bet
I would win, let me show you how I met
A nice girl called Sally Davis.
She's sweet and kind like my mother ole Mavis
And when this war is over we shall win,
If not how will I look after my kin.

So come and fight a hard man's life in the trenches,
We sit for hours on end on the old rotten benches.
They wobble and it stinks bad too,
But you will fight for we need you.

So we say don't be a coward, be a soldier,
For your country we need all the men we can.

And our women can look after the children
And cook upon stoves with the battered pots and pans.

Saffron Willis (12)
Helenswood Upper School, Hastings

It's Not That Bad . . .

Oh, come and welcome, my dear friend!
There's lots of things I need to mend,
Like the creaking door,
Like the freaky floor,
Like the things I made before,
I don't like them, I adore . . . !

Oh, come now, it's not that bad,
Wait until you see Mum,
She is mad!
Although you can only see her nose,
It's not like she already knows,
She's my mummy . . . !

Oh, come now, let's make tea,
You will say, 'How yummy!'
Please ignore the slime and bubbles,
They will taste like lime and rubble . . .

Oh, come now, let's take a walk,
Around the area, we shall talk,
And when we kiss, you shall behold,
The amazing talent I can hold . . .
Of sucking blood!

You look so scared,
Are you freaked out?
Your beautiful mouth,
Stays in a pout.
You can sense the danger, can't you?

You know that I am trying . . .
But can't you tell when I am lying?

Lauren Hughes (12)
Helenswood Upper School, Hastings

After We Came

There's a forest of trees beneath clear blue sky
With brilliant green leaves and trunks of silvered ebony
And others of dusty red bark and lazy, spidering branches
Atop a bright forest floor broken by streams of whispering water
A harmony of silence and bird songs and notes of nature.

After we came, nothing but an empty bag
Fluttering, snagged on the sharp thorns
Of a skeleton tree, standing bent and broken
With whistles of wind speaking of a past it mourns.

Against a rock-covered beach there's a crashing sea
With whirls of green and whirls of dark blue
And foam as white as the salt in the bodies of water,
Teeming with slippery life amidst the murky depths
And creatures crawling to rest beneath the spangled stars.

After we came, everything's changed,
The sea a grey with cans that clatter in all the waves
Beaches full of exported sand, lying in dunes
And no more creatures, just creatures' graves.

Tall mountains stretching as far as the eye can see
Gaping mouths of caves underneath curtains of moss
Topped with the cold white point of snow and clouds
And crumbling dust settling within the crevices that spider up,
Aeons of memories in a natural stone wall.

After we came, the magnificent stone pillars have gone
Covered in buildings that flash with lights
And in the day, crowds of brightly dressed tourists
Scrambling up and littering, spoiling the sights.

After we came, only a few spots are left untouched
All the beauty spoiled in our crush
And as we grow and spread and fill the world we're in,
Nothing will be the same again.

Nadia Daniel (12)
Helenswood Upper School, Hastings

Life's At Steak

Charities, charities, they can be different things,
Some are blessed, and some are sinned,
Some get lots, some get none,
But do we really know, what charities have done?

Breast cancer, Heart Foundation, Hunger in Africa,
These are all charities that matter.

Why don't wars take a break, is there really that much at stake?
Not the steak you have at dinner,
While these poor children get thinner.

I can't understand why you throw away food,
Think of others who aren't as fortunate as you,
The money we spend is extortionate,
Two pounds to give is not that much,
But where it goes is a secret as such.
Our greed has risen high,
And still there they lie.
Can't anyone see?

In some countries children have no rights,
They see horrible things that no child should see,
Some of their family are now deceased,
But there's no time for grieving,
They're lucky they are still breathing.

So keep sitting on that sofa,
Gazing at the TV,
While a child's life is in fear,
Charities will keep working,
Till these horrible causes stop lurking!

Amber Ani (12)
Helenswood Upper School, Hastings

Light And Dark

To never know,
Who will be next?
To never know,
Why I do it.
To never know,
When I'll stop.
To never know,
How many I've killed?
Who I was,
A girl who helped little children from the dark.
Who I was,
Someone who saw the light from the dark.
Who I was,
A friend to many others.
Who I was,
A caring, loving sister.
I will never forget,
As the light faded from their eyes,
I will never forget,
The cries of so many men and women.
I will never forget,
The way this happened to me.
I will never forget,
Why I became this . . .
This barer of life and death.
But I know that now I am this, I can never go back . . .

Natalia Luke (12)
Helenswood Upper School, Hastings

The Real War

Bombs falling like acid rain,
At least I'm not in loads of pain,
Screams and cries from the soldiers below,
I'm stuck here with nowhere to go.

Crying for my family,
They're back at home,
Huddling round the fire,
Together when I'm alone.

Smoke, fire, gas, run,
There goes another son,
Another weeping mother at home,
Because of a letter no one wants to own.

Rousing from the nightmares,
To find no relief,
Trying to calm my thoughts,
And maybe get some sleep.

I see soldiers just like me,
Lying on the ground who couldn't flee,
Cold, grey, red and still,
Who went to the war ready to kill.

So remember the soldiers,
Who lie side by side,
And remember the rest of us,
Who have nowhere to hide.

Cerys Hughes (12)
Helenswood Upper School, Hastings

A Cry Of Sorrow

Colours of dark grey and black fill the world in which she lives in
No other feeling could possibly be worse than this
She sits in a room where there used to be laughter and cheer
Now stands loneliness, emptiness and despair.

Memories of them seem to creep around the corners of my mind
Endless haunting images of your face than won't decline
An overwhelming of emotion that my body can't contain
Fills my soul with unbearable grief, sorrow and pain.

She just sits there waiting for nothing
Even though she doesn't know it's nothing, she can still feel it
Looking out of the window she sees a shadow
Could it be? Of course not, she just has to admit that they're not coming back
Ever.

After time of thinking it through, she gets out of her comfortable position and she finally decided to end it
End it all.
As she walks past her previous life, she thinks all of the thoughts she has thought before
Her vision starts to blur
Death just seems like the only way for her

One last goodbye to her friends, pets and father
As she takes in all the grief
The sorrow of it all hits her hard
One last breath of air
3 . . . 2 . . .

She didn't even get to 1.

Ruby Wilkes
Helenswood Upper School, Hastings

My Black Cat Bobbi!

My black cat Bobbi is very loving,
She calms me when I feel like shoving.
She is calm and she is funny,
And she doesn't need a lot of money.

My black cat Bobbi is very beautiful,
But she is also very unusual.
At times she can be very hyper,
But she doesn't need to wear a diaper.

My black cat Bobbi has a sense of humour,
Fortunately Bobbi doesn't spread rumours.
Sadly my cat is scared of new things,
To me she is better than any kings.

My black cat Bobbi is very weird,
My girl Bobbi doesn't have a beard.
My special cat has cattitude,
And she is always in a good mood.
I love my black cat Bobbi, Miaow.

Leah-Jade Wright (12)
Helenswood Upper School, Hastings

The House Of Terror

The house was damp and dingy,
No sound except the creaky floorboards,
Wonder why no one lived there?
Could it be a monster?
But then I found out with terror!
It was . . .

Paige Birchley (12)
Helenswood Upper School, Hastings

Like Birds Fly

Like birds fly, we run through mud,
Towards a twisted coil of wire,
We trample all life, a flower bud,
And leave in our wake a bloom of fire.

Bodies lie still, stiff, unknown,
Steel rain comes in torrents from the sky,
I stand amongst the fallen alone,
No room for emotion in lifeless eyes.

We live this falsehood deprived of living,
No dignity comes when you finally fall,
Glazed morbid eyes unforgiving,
Until the eerie silence calls.

Like birds fly, we run on forever,
Towards eternal peace and immortality,
We know you grieve but pray together,
Be grateful we no longer suffer reality.

Lucy Bailey (12)
Helenswood Upper School, Hastings

The Witch's Child

Thistles and dandelions
They're my flowers,
Burdock and tangle weed
Blackberries sour,
Rosehips and crab apples
They're my fruit,
Rabbit foot, snake skin
And eye of newt,
Duck's beak and antler
Ground up for a spell,
I am the witch's child,
But I wish you well.

Laura Bullimore (12)
Helenswood Upper School, Hastings

Gas

Gas explodes into the trenches,
Pouring into every nook and cranny,
Seeking them out,
Men running, scrambling, tripping through the massacre.
As they choke on the poisoned air,
An unnatural horror looks them straight in their wild eyes; death.
It seeps out their energy, one by one,
It pollutes their minds,
It deafens their ears, it is unstoppable.
Through the misty night air,
They brush away the branches,
And see a thousand grey ghosts standing by their posts,
Firing,
Firing their screams.
They are invincible, battling through this bombardment unscathed,
Untouchable.
Until finally they falter,
Crumbling into a black void of death.

Annie Marsh (11)
Helenswood Upper School, Hastings

Explosion Of Colour

Flashing images everywhere,
Like powerful lightning bolts.
Explosion of colour takes place,
Enjoyed lots by everyone.

Snap! At the click of a button,
Lasting memory forever.
Big smiles of happiness and glee,
Taken by the camera you see.

Exquisite camera everyone loves,
Pictures, videos,
Everything.
Just for you, whenever you want.

Photography – The magic to make memories.

Anisha Fernando (11)
Helenswood Upper School, Hastings

Where Does Our Money Go?

There is much suffering
In the world.
People, children and animals
Money is spent
Unnecessarily
And much food is wasted,
When will this end?

We donate
For many causes
But do we know
Where our money really goes?
Does it go to those in need?
Or into the pockets
Of those in greed?
People starving to death
They don't even get what's left!
Crying out for little change,
It's time that
Something is arranged.

Like you say
Only £2
Please donate,
Before it becomes too late.

Lily Brash (13)
Helenswood Upper School, Hastings

Absence Makes The Heart Fonder

This life's a nightmare
Got nowhere to run,
Me saying I don't care
People calling me every name under the sun.

Just want my mummy to hold me
Just like we used to be,
Mummy saying she loves me
And me saying, 'It's you and me.'

And when I look in the mirror
I see you,
I'm so proud to be your daughter
Mummy, I love you.

I've got your eyes
I've got your smile,
You were the winning prize
I hope to see you soon in a while.

You can see me from the sky
I never wanted to say goodbye,
You're always in my heart
You were there from the very start.

PS Mummy, I love you.

Stacey Cooper (12)
Helenswood Upper School, Hastings

Snow

Snow, oh how do you flow?

The nice white shine.
Oh just lay, lay, lay! How are you so beautiful?
'Come down,' I shouted, 'never stop.'

Snow, oh how do you flow?

I love your colour, I love your shape and size.
I love how you fall from the sky!
I put my hands out and catch you!
Make snowmen, play snowballs and of course make a snow angel.

Snow, oh how do you flow?

Snow never go lay, lay down.
Snow makes my cheeks glow,
My hands cold.
Doesn't matter, it's all worth it.

Snow, oh how do you flow?

Cäcilia Copland (11)
Helenswood Upper School, Hastings

The Monster

The monster has colourful hair,
The monster has big lips,
The monster has pointy nose,
The monster has massive eyes.

The monster is fat,
The monster is lazy,
The monster is smelly,
The monster is mean.

The monster will eat,
The monster will drink,
The monster will read,
The monster will sleep.

I hate the monster, she's my mummy!

Huda Caglayan (13)
Helenswood Upper School, Hastings

A Lonely Person Who Needs A Mother!

I am a person, who needs a mother,
No one cares or no one bothers.
I am lonely, no one cares,
No one for me or nor will they dare.

Sitting on the streets sleeping, no one to cover me
And when woken up nothing for tea.
A lonely life, do you know what it's like?
It's like wheels fallen off a bike.
I need a mother to care,
Who will hug me like a teddy bear?
Has your mother ever left you?
A lady walking looks like my mother too.

Loneliness is a broken heart,
All you're left with are broken parts.
I don't have a mother, nor do I have a brother.

Who will love me in this world, can you please?

Jarin Islam (12)
Helenswood Upper School, Hastings

Lonely Love

If there is something he can share, it's the love and friendship to all, even in a time of destruction and devastation where the world is at war.

The power of love is indescribable, uncontainable but when he was gone I tried to forget the suffering and the many precious days, for as I shut my eyes I see all.

Through the petrifying pain I see the faces of many as the light of their soul disembarks their body.
So tell me a way to stop the images of death, the only thing that I can see is a bullet through the head.

The power that will thrive through the sadness will scar the hope of the true and fateful.
As there's no greater power, no greater feeling as the love of a lovely child.

Chiara Mills (11)
Helenswood Upper School, Hastings

War Poem

Why was everyone running?
What was coming?
Help . . . help . . . help . . .
The stench of gunfire hung heavily in the air,
Caught here like a trembling animal awaiting the snare.
He needed help,
There goes another yelp.
Help . . . help . . . help . . .
As I make sense of the situation, enveloped in fear,
The reality, was becoming all too clear.
Everyone now letting out a shout,
He was in trouble no doubt.
We all were.

Megan Boles (11)
Helenswood Upper School, Hastings

A Day In A Lab

The amount of animals being used,
Just for products that we use;
Rabbits, hamsters even cats,
All sitting waiting on their mats
Wishing they could run and play,
Without shampoo in their eyes all day.

People say it's only some,
But every hamster must have fun.
Cats should sit by the fire and purr
And not have hand-cream in their fur.
Rabbits should be hopping free,
So please, please stop this cruelty.

Felicity Woodfine (13)
Helenswood Upper School, Hastings

World War Three

There's nothing left of the world now,
Russia, America, England or Hastings,
Just grey, brown and sooty black,
Now there's no bringing home back.

With all the weapons, bombs and nuclear explosions,
There's whole streets left, whole streets destroyed,
Uniformed wooden shacks for people to sleep,
The murky holes in the earth are really deep.

I stumble onto the beach or what's left of it,
Just the vast ocean stained ruby red,
But the sea still arches his back,
He doesn't want to start an attack.

I creep through the old town and duck from the debris,
Remember pressing my face against the windows,
Now the glass is shattered on the grey floor.
Now I can't press my nose there anymore.

I turn around and gape at the place,
Where my school used to proudly stand,
The lessons and the teachers, who were inspiring,
The strong school spirit is now expiring.

As I stand and sob like a waterfall,
The dismal rain pours down on Hastings,
The rain can't wash away my sorrow,
When I don't even know if there will be a tomorrow.

There's nothing left of the world now,
Russia, America, England or Hastings,
Just grey, brown and sooty black,
Now there's no bringing home back.

Lillie Brett (13)
Helenswood Upper School, Hastings

The Piper

The music swirls and dances
As he sways
It twists and bends
Like flowing ribbons of sound
You sway,
As he captures you in his web of sound
The rhythm wraps around you
It twists through your body,
He starts to march
And you follow enchanted in his trance
You start to dance as he leads you,
Your cares forgotten
As his music pulls you
Completely enchanted,
The world slips away over your head
He leads you . . .
. . . Leads you . . .
. . . Leads you . . .

Lucrezia MacDonald (11)
Helenswood Upper School, Hastings

Drugs

Hello my name is Drugs – I destroy homes,
Tear families apart and that's just the start!
I'm more costly than diamonds, more costly than gold,
The sorrow I bring is a sight to behold.
And if you need me, remember I'm easily found,
I live all around you in schools and in town.
I live with the rich; I live with the poor,
I live down the street or even next door.
My power is awesome; try me you'll see,
But if you do, you may never break free!
Just try me once and I may let you go,
But try me twice and I'll own your soul.
When I possess you, you'll steal and you'll lie.
You do what you have to just to get high.
The crimes you'll commit, for my narcotic charms,
Will be worth the pleasure you'll feel in your arms.
You'll lie to your mum; you'll steal from your dad,
When you see their tears you should feel sad.
But you'll forget your morals and how you were raised,
I'll be your consequence, I'll teach you my ways.
I take kids from parents; I take parents from kids
I'll take everything from you, your looks and your pride,
I'll be right by your side.
You'll give up everything . . . your family, your home,
Your friends and your money then you'll be all alone.
I'll take and take till you have nothing more to give,
When I've finished with you you'll be lucky to live!
The nightmares I'll give you when lying in bed,
The voices you'll hear from inside your head,
The sweats, the shakes, and the visions you'll see;
I want you to know these are all gifts from me.
You'll regret that you tried me, try always do,
But you came to me, I not to you.
You could have just said no and walked away,

If you could live that day over, what would you say?
I'll be your master; you'll be my slave,
I'll even go with you, when you go to your grave.
I can bring you more misery than words can tell,
Come take my hand and I'll lead you to Hell.

Megan Keesing (12)
Helenswood Upper School, Hastings

Is Someone Out There?

Child abuse is something I detest
There are those poor children
Who have been picked from the rest.

They are quiet, shy and
Don't always cry,
Their feelings they keep inside
For many their love is denied.

This abuse needs to cease
With much help form the police
Social services and authorities too,
I could help, they could help
And maybe you.

When a child is withdrawn
Looking forlorn and may not be able to cry
Just look at the bruises for silence it chooses,
Those questions need answering and why?

Madina Zaynudinova (12)
Helenswood Upper School, Hastings

I Hate War

With my machine gun in my hands,
I sprint across the red, sticky street.
Sweat dripping down my head,
All I can hear is my heartbeat.

A merciless man,
Put a gun to an innocent man's head.
And as quick as a blink,
. . . He's dead.

People scatter in every direction,
Crying with absolute fear.
Like dogs trying to find their owner,
It brings to my eyes a tear.

I have been instructed,
To kill every civilian I see.
I'm not sure if this,
Is the man I want to be.

Corpses are kicked aside by soldiers,
As if they're sacks of sand.
And all I can see,
Is the destruction of the land.

Should I back out?
And leave this place for good?
Or would I have to face the consequences?
I probably would.

In the corner of my eye,
I catch a glimpse of a small, dirty child.
I cannot face killing her,
So instead I tell her to hide.

She shakes her head stubbornly,
Then starts to suck her thumb.
But then her ears prick up and her eyes open wide,
And she points over to her mum.

I turn around to see a woman,
With a gun held to her head.
She refuses to speak, so with a bang,
She collapses to the floor,
Dead.

I cannot bear to watch,
All I can hear is a child's wail,
The tiny footsteps of running to her mother,
A bang . . .

Silence.

Izzy Catterall (14)
Helenswood Upper School, Hastings

Would You Choose War?

Flame propelled shrapnel consuming the light,
Nothing but blood, wire and fire in sight.
But the passion fuelled tiger pierces the mist,
Despite his threat he still persists . . .

'For kingdom, for country,' blasts the inferior man.
Nothing but fate will script his plan,
Bullets flying from left to right,
The remains of soldiers, who have had their last fight.

His trousers mudded to the knee,
His eyes unable to, past five foot see.
His cammo and ammo, both useless as each other
(Not when you're incapable of reaching cover.)

Shadows defined by the bullets, muzzle flash,
To dare try fire, means his life he would cash,
So sound and much movement he's careful to shoo,
If it is his life he values!

But the brave, the fearless and the scarred prevail,
But no one passes nor do they fail.
For dying is the alternative to a life not to implore,
A life you and I know as war.

Amber Pearson (12)
Helenswood Upper School, Hastings

Nothing

There is none to work for,
So nothing to be paid,
Nothing to do on this cold winter's day,
There is nothing to do,
Nothing to play,
Not much to say on this cold winter's day,
There is nothing to eat,
Nothing to watch.

The cold's making Dad mad he can't go outside,
And Mum is worried she will slip on the ice,
The mice are outside having fun a while,
I am in here with my mum.

There is nothing to read,
Nothing to write,
But,
There is one thing to say,
There is absolutely nothing to do today.

Sophie Chappell (11)
Helenswood Upper School, Hastings

Death Field

The sound of the war drums cry;
As my positivity slowly slips away.
The massacred corpses; congesting the death field approach,
Their ghosts passing me by.
My trepidation increases with every step,
My trusty steed takes.

The daredevil Germans advance up ahead,
Then through the deafening silence,
I hear the one word I dreaded most:
Charge!

The blizzard of shells flying through the air like a swarm of deadly wasps.
As we charge into the ghastly battle,
I embrace my stallion in hope to survive;
And I whisper, 'We will make it together!'

We canter through,
With hope of survival.
As the stench of rotten flesh fills my nose,
And the screams of the dead echo around me.
Will this fate befall on me?

The sound of the war drums cry;
As my positivity slowly slips away.
The massacred corpses congesting the death field approach,
Their ghosts passing me by.
My trepidation increases with every step,
My trusty steed takes.

Jessica Fisher (13)
Helenswood Upper School, Hastings

Giraffe

The giraffe moved gracefully through the trees. Extending his long neck, he ate the juicy branches, using his black tongue hanging out of his mouth.

Giraffe ran towards his opponent, still proudly placing his delicate hooves on the dusty ground. Then the opponent took the first move, powerfully bashing the giraffe's neck. He then took his move. They carried on, through the night, their bodies rippling in the moonlight.

The giraffe saw the girl. He walked over to her. She looked slightly dishevelled, but the giraffe did not notice. He thought her slender figure looked elegant. He came close, as silent as the wind. She acknowledged him and then advanced to him. As the sun set, they watched it, grateful for each other.

The giraffe noticed him creeping up in the tree. No one could deceive his eagle eyes. The leopard was coming towards his head. He could catch him easily if he stayed where he was. So he ran. The leopard never caught him.

Giraffes are long. When they eat they use their long tongue. When they fight, they use their long neck. When they love, they use their long faces for affection. When they run, they use their long legs.

Giraffe.

Alice Jenner (11)
Helenswood Upper School, Hastings

Stormy Night

A storm was a brewing when he cycled by
He had no place to stay,
People pointed to the sky
He had to get away.

The icy rain began to fall
He wished he was at home,
A lady called him from her door
'No need for you to roam.'

She led him in and kept him dry
He warmed up by the fire
And soon enough she served him up
A steaming plate of pie.

That night as he lay warm in bed
The storm outside did scream,
So glad he was to be inside
Drifting towards sweet dreams.

Lucy Smith (11)
Helenswood Upper School, Hastings

They Come And Go!

(Does anyone care!)
They go every day,
Without having a say,
To the lab to be tested and doped,
They don't get a chance to walk, run or play,
It is a case of which ones have coped.

They sit in cages and wait all day,
Wishing they could go out and play,
Perfume, shampoo is dropped in their eyes, it is finding out those ones who will cry,
A tiny mouse develops a rash,
It's suffered an experiment for lots of cash,
A man in the lab has put it to sleep,
Occasionally it's death;
There's no time to weep.

Years have gone by,
And thousands have died,
For all these experiments loads of people have lied
It's wrong!

Megan Hughes (13)
Helenswood Upper School, Hastings

Please No More War

All those loved ones
On the ground.
All that's heard,
A moaning sound.
All those loved ones
On the floor, all the wives
Behind shut doors.

Mum says it's going to be alright,
But she's always sitting up all night.
She didn't want him to go,
In the fear that he won't come
Home.

'Please don't let Daddy go,' I cried,
Mother said we will be fine.
'What if Daddy dies out there?'
'He'll be fine,' she screamed and into the distance she stared.
Is it fair we have to wait,
The pain and sorrow for our mate?
Is it fair we don't know?
We might have just lost a soul . . .

Rebecca Hate (12)
Helenswood Upper School, Hastings

Death

Death is a cloak, worn by the man,
The man with a will to do what he can,
He takes your life and throws it away,
No point in hiding, he'll get you someday.

His bones, they chatter under the breeze,
The deadly sight, drops you to your knees,
With nowhere to run and nowhere to hide,
You'll rot and wither from deep inside.

Once you've seen him there's no going back,
As you take a trip down the lifeless track,
Deep in the heart, a black abyss,
No going back, you won't exist.

A tear for sorrow, one lost love,
No longer free, trapped like a dove,
The family you will leave behind,
As daunting memories cross your mind.

Death is a cloak, worn by the man,
A man with the will to do what he can,
Deep in the heart, a black abyss,
No coming back, you won't be missed.

Bethany Williams (13)
Helenswood Upper School, Hastings

Little Amy Lou

This is a poem
About Amy Lou
Who never wanted to be abused.

Her dad was a drunk
Her mum was an addict,
They kept little Amy
Locked in an attic.

She walked to school thinking no one cared
Wearing the same dress as yesterday,
But with a new bruise upon her face.

Her daddy comes home angry
She runs away and hides,
Crying for the beating tonight.

The school were worried
She didn't come to school,
They called social services
To knock on the door.

No answer
No reply
Except little Amy's last cry.

Caitlin Mann (13)
Helenswood Upper School, Hastings

I Didn't

I didn't do this,
I didn't do that,
I didn't drop the baby,
I didn't kick the cat,
I didn't break the windows,
I didn't steal the phone,
I didn't eat the sweets,
I didn't moan and groan,
I didn't hide the chocolate,
I didn't pull rude faces,
I didn't rip up the book,
I didn't cheat in races.
I didn't break the tap,
I didn't make the mess,
I didn't squash the ant,
I didn't stain Mum's dress,
I didn't drop the mug,
I didn't spill the tea,
I didn't break the rules,
It was him, not me!

Evie Taylor (11)
Moira House School, Eastbourne

Snowflakes

So soft and pure, you gently fall around
I watch you through my window every day,
So white and gleaming as you float to ground.
You make me so cheerful in every way,
I play with you in morning, noon and night,
In winter is the time you come to dance
Some days the awful rain gives you a fright,
But then you come with me and we do prance.
I love you so and you do love me back,
You bury me in wonderful white snow
In which I frolic, laugh and snow I stack,
But after days it's time for you to go.

I wish there's somewhere else that I could be,
I wonder when you will come back to me . . .

Helen Grout (12)
Moira House School, Eastbourne

Marmite

Oh my, you are so heavenly and yum,
Yes I could cry for your sweet embrace,
You feel so good, deep in my hungry tum,
And I don't think you are a bad disgrace,

And how can I explain the ugly taste,
It puts a horrible frown upon my face,
And on my tongue it feels like fish paste,
It is so bad, I think it is from space,

But I cannot make up my mind today,
Do I love it or hate it, I can't think,
One day I want it to go far away,
The next I want to eat it in a blink.

Do I love it or hate it help, please help,
I don't know what to do and I will, yelp!

Olivia Beale (12)
Moira House School, Eastbourne

Gone

It happened so fast,
As if in a blink,
One day you were there,
Now what do you think?
It was terrifying and oh so quick,
Like a break of a glass,
Like a snap of a twig,
The silence was deafening,
No breath from your lips,
A stolen crown jewel; a treasure so missed.

Amelia Carrington (12)
Moira House School, Eastbourne

Fox Hunting

Foxes should not be hunted
Foxes have a right to rule,
This shouldn't be happening,
I find it very cruel.

Foxes' lives should be spared,
Mercy to them you should give,
Don't let foxes leave this world,
Foxes deserve to live!

Foxes are amazing
Don't be really bad,
If you don't hunt them,
We'll be very glad.

Please don't kill the foxes
Don't be a twit,
So if you see a fox,
Don't kill it!

Dominic Hanley (11)
Oaklands Catholic School, Portsmouth

A Victorious Score

Fans flocked for miles to see the game,
Chelsea Football Club versus Tottenham again!
The crowd went wild at the whistle sound,
And eruption of noise flew from the ground,
Soon, half time came by,
A victory was nigh!
The second half saw Tottenham's aim breached,
However . . . Chelsea's aim was reached.
5-1 a victorious score,
It's safe to say their play was not poor!

Ted Wells (13)
Oaklands Catholic School, Portsmouth

The Real World!

Why does this happen?
People are careless,
Think about nothing other than themselves,
Heartless people are in sight!

Just for their fur,
Just for their meat,
They're becoming more extinct,
It's hardly something they live for!

Numbers, numbers,
They're becoming low,
By the time they all go,
They'll just be an old sight or glow.

How can we stop this?
How can this go?
It's just a matter of time,
Or for someone to know!

Seren Evans (12)
Oaklands Catholic School, Portsmouth

You're Beautiful

Being disabled it's not a crime.
When you ask and they don't give you the time,
Caterpillars waiting to come out of their cocoon
And they're no different to me or you.

When you see them and stare
There's no need they know they're there
They don't understand why
And it's way too unfair

They are unique in every way,
Even when they have nothing to say
They mean words that have so much effect,
Nobody's perfect, but everyone is beautiful
You're beautiful . . .

Chloe Line (13)
Oaklands Catholic School, Portsmouth

Hockey

Hockey is a game of two halves,
It really, really aches your calves.
Football's over rated, hockey's under dated!

Hit it smack in the back of the net and score a goal without a sweat,
The kit won't get dirty on an Astroturf, so the kids don't end up covered in earth,
With a club house nearby,
Warm and cosy so you won't look like a blue Smurf.

Smacking balls at 60 miles an hour, zoom boom bam across the pitch,
In the air on the ground it doesn't matter how they get there,
But as long as the umpire's sure.

It won't make you rich like Alan Sugar, but it will be fun and you'll have a good run.

Luke Ellul Turner (13)
Oaklands Catholic School, Portsmouth

Beautiful Birds

Beautiful birds, wonderful birds
Singing their song in my ears,
Flying up high, touching the sky
Leaving my eyes full of tears.

Flying around, feeding the young
Collecting food for their chicks
Gathering feathers for their home,
Their nest made entirely of sticks.

I've always loved birds, ever since I was two,
Flying to the heavens above
Dropping their fluff, caught by the wind,
Pigeon, finch and dove.

Birds protect their young from the bad,
Knowing they have time on this earth,
Telling them to hide, value their life,
While they give back all that they're worth.

I value all birds, love them to death
I feed them all the bread I can find,
If they are chased away, I won't like that at all
And give them a piece of my mind

Water birds, flying birds
Even ones that can't fly!
All sing their song, their wonderful song,
Beautiful birds, I hate them to die.

The early bird catches the worm, or so that's what they say
But I don't think that is true,
As I hear so many tweeting at the start of the day!

Sophie Hanley (11)
Oaklands Catholic School, Portsmouth

Imagine

Imagine waking up exhausted,
And imagine waking up cold.
No family, no friends, no bed, no sleep,
Just the clothes on your back,
Just the clothes on your feet,
And an angry hunger that's uncontrolled.

Imagine having no fresh water,
To gently pour from the tap;
Nothing to quench, nothing to cleanse,
Just dry land stretching outward,
Just a blur in the distance a mirage, could send,
When under the scorching sun you're trapped.

Imagine living in fear,
Where your mind would be playing tricks,
Because you have no shelter or safety,
Just enough energy for living,
Just enough for hoping, 'Don't kill me'
And hoping the war will soon cease to exist.

Once they're tackled by the root,
These injustices can at last be suppressed,
No longer branching issues from the tree.
What once was poverty; absolute and relative,
What once was man-made or occurred naturally,
Can be prevented, and reduced, not just digressed.

When we see through our hearts,
And beyond our deceiving eyes,
We can imagine equality and hope,
Just in our reach with patience,
Just creating a world that would cope,
To silence and comfort its last cries.

Nicole Crosbourne (16)
Oaklands Catholic School, Portsmouth

I Can't Write Poems

I can't write poems
I'm not going to lie,
Unlike some people
Even though we are equal.

I am not a poet
But neither are you,
But we still do it
Because we never knew.

I am Welsh
And like sheep,
I know right
It's a stereotype.

After reading this
I'm sure you'll know,
I can't write poems
But at least I admit it.

Alec Clapp (14)
Oaklands Catholic School, Portsmouth

Young Carer

Some people point,
Some people stare,
People laugh and call them names,
Little do they know it causes them pain.

Do they care?
It's just not fair!
They are just human inside,
Look with your heart not your eye.

You may be thinking, *so?*
But little do you know,
Their families spend their lives
Trying to help and provide,
Their child with a normal life,
Even though they might never have kids or a wife.

You may be thinking, *so?*
But little do they know,
That I am a member,
I am a young carer.

Chloe Harding (13)
Oaklands Catholic School, Portsmouth

What Is Happening To Us All?

There was once a time when people used to live in luxury,
Ornaments were made of diamonds and gold,
Houses were built to the size of basketball courts,
Where people used to drive Benz and Bentleys,
But all of this changed,
Two years ago.
The Syrian war had taken all they ever had,
Where once people used to freely roam,
Now are afraid to take a step,
The houses where they lived are nothing but thoughts,
When darkness takes over, their safety becomes a priority.

Many do not know how it feels to have a gun pointed at their body,
Where once the sky was blue now is a dark grey,
The people only wish for this to end but how many dead, only God knows.

Those who seek freedom, we say to them, 'Be patient,'
Those who support the leader, we say stop this war now!
How does he not realise that he was one of those a few dreams ago.
So then let me ask all of you one question:
What is happening to us all?

Joel Mathew (13)
Oaklands Catholic School, Portsmouth

Never Stop!

Never stop caring about the little things in life,
Never stop dreaming or give in to strife,
Never stop wondering, if you are on your own,
Never stop believing that you're the greatest, and everyone knows.

Jack Seymour (14)
Oaklands Catholic School, Portsmouth

Fitting In

I smoke to be 'indie'
I drink to 'fit in'
Still no one likes me,
Why am I a din?

My 'friends' think I'm fat,
My dad thinks I'm gay,
I shall soon be popular
Just give me a day?

If I was just popular,
Just for one week,
I could show the world
That I'm not just some geek.

If I was just skinny
I would try to keep it that way,
Then maybe just maybe
My dad would believe I'm not gay.

Why do I smoke?
Why do I drink?
Why oh why
Don't just stop . . . and think?

I will not be fat,
I will not be gay,
The smoking and drinking
Will stop . . . today!

Josh Smith (13)
Oaklands Catholic School, Portsmouth

Reading Is The Key

Reading is the key to the
Door we call our mind,
Find out for yourself,
Come and look inside.
Reading is the key to adventure,
Mystery and much more,
Pick up a book now and
Let your mind soar.
Reading is the key to whom we
Once were and what we will be,
If you don't believe me open
Your eyes and you will see.
Reading is the key to intelligence,
Giving you what you gained but lost,
Also giving you the ability to learn
Something new at no extra cost.
Reading is the key to emotions
Showing us what we know about
Ourselves and what we don't, also
It helps understand others on a new note.
Reading is the key to life itself,
Setting free the wonders that are confined,
Come on now, hurry up and travel to
The reading world that awaits you!

Michael Salloum (14)
Oaklands Catholic School, Portsmouth

I Want My Say!

The world is busy,
Politicians arguing,
Shouting themselves dizzy.

The world is crazy,
Teaching shouting,
They'll tell you off if you're lazy.

The world is controlled
By adults in charge,
Telling children to do what they're told.

Children need their say
They can think,
Can't they?

Children need their say
They have ideas
Don't they?

If you are an adult,
Teacher, parent, leader,
Don't squash, squish and squeeze
Children into a hole,

Let them be free and
Have their say!

Judy Quinn (12)
Oaklands Catholic School, Portsmouth

Football Is Great

Football is great,
Hosts the second biggest sporting event,
Holds great teams,
Liverpool, Barcelona, AC Milan,
Some of the greats.

Talented players all over the show,
Even though it holds racism and cheats,
However football is as important as breathing,
Some say.

But football is loved where ever you go,
So if you dislike football you are missing out,
Football is a must-be part of life,
Football is great.

Matt Knight (13)
Oakland Catholic School, Portsmouth

Stereotyping

We seek knowledge in our everyday lives,
Abuse eating us away.
Racism, prejudice, is this really okay?

Judging a man plainly by his differences, are these really the footsteps we are set to follow?
Or are our hearts just maybe too hollow?
We must follow Jesus; teach others His way,
Or will this madness keep spreading like tooth decay?

Alfred Johnston (13)
Oaklands Catholic School, Portsmouth

Untitled

Poland fell in 1939
Britain went to war
Germany captured French work,
People were hungry,

Food was low, people forced to work,
In despair they have no hope
Under Nazi control they are scared, terrified of dying.

German bomber flew over Britain
Bombs dropping, it was a loud sound.
Shock over Britain's people
Fire spread over Britain
Fireman trying to put out deadly blaze.

Britain fight back with bombs over Germany
Germany suffered with heavy loss and lots of buildings destroyed
War is coming to end, soon for people to live in peace
Russia invade Berlin, conquer it and Nazi party members committed suicide
War has come to the end, peace is now around the world for the people live a normal life.

Daniel Keith (16)
Osborne School, Winchester

Iron Man

Iron Man is a strong, kind, good and a nice man in a suit of armour.

He is also a strict, careful, fast, steady, powerful, muscly and funny man.

Iron Man has an echoy voice when he talks in his armour.

Iron Man is calm when it comes to a bad situation.

Iron Man's armour is mechanical, robotic and with rays so powerful they could turn you to dust.

It is a mystery who he really is in public.

Kevin Bennett (16)
Osborne School, Winchester

The Right Of Young People

There once was a boy called Jim, he was seven,
And had black, scruffy hair and smelly scruffy clothes.
Dirty face, hungry belly, not cared for,
His mum and dad don't care for him.
He is not loved.

At school, can't concentrate, hungry all the time,
Sad, unloved, uncared for Jim.
They should look after him.
He asks them why they don't care?
They don't know, they don't have answers
Too busy to notice, too busy to care.

Jim is given another family.
One who cares.
They love him, they feed him
They clean his clothes,
He can have a better life.

Sean Boland (16)
Osborne School, Winchester

The Dancing Poem

When I start to dance, I feel happy,
Like a floating bird in the sky.
Shining like a diamond in the shimmery blue,
Rising out of view.

Spinning round, the faces blur,
The people jump off their seats like blasting rockets
The crowd was loud like an erupting volcano
The crowd was amazing like a tiny sun
The costumes were shining like a glitter ball
The sequins were sparkling like a starry sky.

Zoe Grace Birmingham (15)
Osborne School, Winchester

About My Degu, Socks

Socks, Socks, my little Socks,
So sweet just like homemade honey,
Your fur so soft like a soft peach,
Every time I cuddle you, your heart warms up mine.

Socks you held on strong till you could,
But sadly nature took its toll.
Me and your brother Buttons we will always miss you,
Us three were like chalk and cheese.

Now it only feels like the chalk,
We will miss you Socks,
Your kind and gentle kindness,
Always helps me to get through the day,
RIP Socks.

Stefan Nicholson (16)
Osborne School, Winchester

Complete Comedy

Comedy is like my family,
Some makes me laugh
Some makes me cry laughing,
But the feeling inside of me,
Makes me feel like I'm in
Heaven, full of beautiful angels
Swaying side by side on soft
Cuddly clouds and rainbow
Pattern butterflies, fluttering
Through the warm, cosy air,
That's what comedy feels like
To me, comedy completes the
Pieces of my heart.

Jerry Almeida (16)
Osborne School, Winchester

My Family

I love my family because they are special to me.
I love my mum and she always makes me a lovely dinner.
I love my dad because he helps me with my homework.
I love my sister Isabelle and I like to say good morning to her.
I love my brother, I like to make him cups of tea.
I love my nephew because he is my best friend.
I love my sister Gemma because she is kind to me.

Tom Greer (15)
Osborne School, Winchester

I Don't Like Dancing

I really don't like dancing
It makes me feel embarrassed,
I really don't like dancing
In front of lots of people.

Dancing is not my type of hobby
It doesn't make me happy inside,
It makes me feel really angry and upset
I really do not like to dance.

The costumes look really silly
They are really old and far too frilly
I really don't like wearing tap shoes
They are really tight and far too noisy.

Overall it really is so tiring
I don't like dancing
It's such hard work!

Kyel Climo (16)
Osborne School, Winchester

The Bus

On the bus it has no radio,
But we don't need a radio,
Because we have a laugh and joke.
Our bus breaks down,
Our driver Chris gets cross.

We have a race with
Mick on Osborne 4,
To get to school first
Mick always wins,
I call him Lord Smirky
And the Escort is a Smirkett.

The bus always breaks down,
The tail lift is old and rusty,
It never lets the wheelchairs in
And they get stuck in the driveways,
This makes us late.

Tom Williams (16)
Osborne School, Winchester

My Girlfriend

My girlfriend is beautiful,
I love my girlfriend so much,
My girlfriend is lovely,
My girlfriend is gorgeous.

My girlfriend has big beautiful eyes,
She makes me feel very happy inside,
She has very pretty long blonde hair,
She smells like flowers and the summer.

She is kind and funny,
She is lovely and cuddly,
She is my best friend,
I really love my girlfriend.

Kelan Burrows (15)
Osborne School, Winchester

Snow Day

The special snow fell from the sky on Saturday.
There were snowmen standing still by the swings.
There was a slug in the snow as well.
Something was silly.

Cameron Hammond (13)
Osborne School, Winchester

I Hate School

I really hate school,
I really hate learning,
My teacher is horrible,
She makes me work,
She knows I hate working.

Teacher, I want to go home now,
I want to be at home right now,
I want to be with my nanny,
I want to sit on the sofa and eat,
Teacher knows I hate doing work.

I really hate school.
I want to go home,
I don't want to do work,
I don't want homework,
I want to be sat on the sofa watching TV.

George Metters (16)
Osborne School, Winchester

Never Again

There was a lifeless, crippled body,
Dangling from a roof top,
Its head nowhere to be seen,
For it was the morning after the night where it had all started.

The streets were empty, sand blowing around,
Silence haunted the surroundings for miles,
Until that one sound that played, haunting the streets for miles –
The one sound that this country awaits every second of every day,
To prove its loyalty through its religion,
The middle-east Arabian music that sweeps the whole place with belief.

The one point where we can retreat,
Get away from the massacre,
The horrified soldiers that are scarred for life,
Make their journey back before unimaginable madness occurs once again.

But, time ran short,
For their journey back from madness did not in fact succeed.
As the music stopped the horror occurred once again,
The bullet driven ground collected them one by one.

They will never be found for the ground claims them,
Only to be discovered when time decides,
Their lives cut short,
Never again!

Lauren Jennion (15)
Peacehaven Community School, Peacehaven

The Hallway

The hallway, oh hallway, keeps going on.
The hallway, oh hallway, dark as black paint.
The hallway, oh hallway is very long.
The hallway, oh hallway, makes you just faint.

The screams, oh screams for the hallway they shout.
The screams, oh screams from the people they yell.
The screams, screams you don't want to hang about.
The screams, oh screams they sound like they're from Hell.

Many people never come out from there.
Who knows what's ahead, maybe a quick scare.
The hallway is now lit with many flares.
The stories are told sitting on a chair.

The horrible monster, many will see.
You may not realise, this monster is me.

Dylan Mayers (12)
Peacehaven Community School, Peacehaven

I Do

From the best first day I met you, I knew,
And I have always wanted to confess,
That I want to spend my future with you,
As your one and only golden goddess,
The day I brought up the courage was good,
And I will never, ever regret it,
Although my friends always say I should,
From that minute we were the perfect fit,
Without him I feel so very alone,
Also a little bit like I am cold,
Like bluey ice cream in an ice cream cone,
I want his warm heart in a lovely mould,
The thing is I will not always be new,
In this moment right now I say . . . *I do!*

Milly Usher-Wheatley (12)
Peacehaven Community School, Peacehaven

Six Nations

Through mud and white lines
We will fight
Our hands and our boots
With our might
Blood, sweat and courage
We will brawl
We are one we are strong
We will maul
For each other and for self
We will drive
We have trained all our lives
We will thrive
Lay our bodies on the line
With hearts of gold
Our actions seal our fate
We will stand

Five will fall.

Jimmy Evans (16)
Peacehaven Community School, Peacehaven

News

Tar crawls up,
Bubbling,
Into their tyrannical fire.
Babbling,
The crowd screams.
Another child falls down, blood, from the nose,
Cameras crawl up.
Two days later the reporter indifferent, bored,
'There are no more casualties.'
The sadistic anticipation cut down,
'No more casualties.'
We try not to feel disappointed.

Harry Kingscote (16)
Peacehaven Community School, Peacehaven

Love Yourself

Don't take models as inspiration,
They're not as perfect as they seem,
Making you notice your imperfections,
And crushing down your self esteem.

Think that you are worthless,
And hating the skin you're in,
Piling on makeup day after day,
And starving until you're thin.

To finally start to love yourself,
You must forget this feeling so blue,
Taking care of yourself and keeping your health,
And remembering you are you.

Forget trying to look doll like,
And push that dream afar,
Because you're already perfect,
Just the way you are.

Abigail Dunkerton (12)
Peacehaven Community School, Peacehaven

Summertime Beauty

I cannot wait for summertime to come,
To feel the warm breeze in my flowing hair,
To feel my warm cheek on the burning sun,
Run barefoot on the grass without a care,
To bathe in the sun and bathe in the sea,
To ride on a donkey upon the beach,
Oh what a beautiful day this will be!
Sit in the garden and enjoy a peach,
To sit on a tree trunk and read a book,
To throw your head back, the sun on your face,
To climb a tall tree and take a look,
To sleep under the stars they have such grace,
At the end the roses fade away,
And the animals hide away and stay.

Izzi Vaughan (12)
Peacehaven Community School, Peacehaven

To Milo

There are many things I love about you,
Such as your delicate black and white fur,
The way it makes me call you my moo moo,
Your eyes are the colour of spiky burrs.

Your really weird diet, the food you eat,
Your pink nose looks kind of like a berry.
Our races down the stairs; it's me you beat,
The way you like to purr to be merry.

The way your white claws are sharp like a knife,
The way you chase me when I've got a tart,
The way your tail helps you balance in life,
You are so friendly; you've got a kind heart.

You always hug me whenever I get up,
I love when you try to drink from a cup.

Amber Harrington (12)
Peacehaven Community School, Peacehaven

Family

Love is unconditional; Mummy dear,
Your hair is a gorgeously, lovely brown,
I'm with Dad and you are always so near,
You're gorgeous like the sun even when down.

My dad is amazing; he makes my life,
His hair, his eyes, his laugh, his jokes; everything,
You always say you love me and your wife,
Our hugs make me happy and when you sing.

My great bro and sis also make my life,
I don't know what I would do without them,
They always, always help me with my strife,
And to me they are my great precious gems.

We may be different, but I do love them,
But we girls outnumber all of the men!

Kristal Alice Philpot (12)
Peacehaven Community School, Peacehaven

Snake, Snake

Snake, snake.
Like a long rake,
Snake, snake,
Don't put it in a cake,
Snake, snake,
For goodness sake,
Snake, snake,
They make me shake,
Snake, snake,
I called him Jake,
Snake, snake,
Or maybe Drake,
Snake, snake,
He keeps me awake,
Snake, snake,
He makes my skin flake,
Snake, snake,
My snake fought a snake,
Snake, snake,
It was a big mistake.
Because he died.

Luke Knight (15)
Peacehaven Community School, Peacehaven

Forgotten

The screaming sound of falling souls,
And the booming sight of wretched foes,
Way out there in no-man's-land,
I'm sure I've been forgotten.

The toxic gas storming the trench,
The smell of death providing a vile stench,
Way out here in no-man's-land,
I'm sure I've been forgotten.

The laughing winds and stormy seas,
Where everyone cries, all but me,
Way out here in no-man's-land,
I'm sure I've been forgotten.

Taking my last breath,
Taking a forever rest,
Our name is up in fame,
We will never be forgotten . . .

Matthew Hooper (15)
Peacehaven Community School, Peacehaven

Untitled

I disinclined through the shadows of destructive giants,
Of those wounded soldiers that were so reliant,
My love,
The bloodshed tears cascaded
Past his cheek
Became pointless,
Worthless and dry, the tears of a lifeless soldier,
My love.
Traumatised citizens watch in terror as dangling tendons saturated.
The spurting of blood detach from the remainder of his body,
My love.
The breaking of minds sharpens, piercing my fragile ears,
The acrid smoke spreads as the tears poor from,
My love.
The horror, terror, a valour.
How can I help? How can I cure the wounded man? How can I help
My love?

Ruby Eisnor (16)
Peacehaven Community School, Peacehaven

Two

Heat rushing.
Face blushing.
Debris crushing.
Souls . . . flushing,
Away, away.
Distant cries.
Not even flies,
Grace the skin that fries.
They cry. They try
To fly but just . . . die.

And the families – a representation of the horror.
The tragedies – blemishes upon the map, the graves filling.
The eyes – together these images, imprinting on their brains.
The lives – clasped upon with a firm grip, wrenched down. And down. And down.

These were
Just two numbers, irrelevant before,
Just two numbers, now remembered, forever and more.

Elliot Windsor (15)
Peacehaven Community School, Peacehaven

Conflict

I hear the anger,
The screams of innocent children,
Their cries of help echoing in my head,
I see rubble and carcasses sprawled on the ground.

I smell the smoke from the bombs,
The smell of fear fresh in the air,
I see strands of hair,
Falling like torrential rain,

I see bullets laid out on the ground covered in blood,
Like a mini flood,
I feel the grief of a victim's family,
In far away valleys,

My heart pounding rapidly,
While I stood there and gasped,
At the dead bodies that lay in front of me,

I am in conflict . . .

Adam Stenning (16)
Peacehaven Community School, Peacehaven

War

Shut the blinds,
'Mummy, why are you covering your eyes?'
– Silence.

She stills,
He's fighting for her, he'll keep them safe.
Hope.

Tear stains,
Pen to paper water vapour, her therapy.
– Helps.

It's sent,
Her post office possesses all he needs,
Wants.

It's over,
She feels relief and pure happiness.
Finally.

But alas,
She speaks too soon as the tornados fire,
Gone.

Ruby Gislingham (16)
Peacehaven Community School, Peacehaven

The Music Sonnet

Music, music, music, I love to sing
My best lesson, my teacher Mr Browne,
Microphones, I like you use, oh that thing!
Keyboards, not too sure, but I never frown,
I really like music it makes me smile,
When a band is playing it can smile too,
It can flow so much like the River Nile,
So many instruments that are brand new,
Trumpets, keyboards and drums so many more,
The trombone and guitar, the violin,
And I always stick next to the music door,
I hear a minim note and don't ignore,
Someday I hope it is not very far,
That I might soon become a music star!

Jasmine Thorpe (11)
Peacehaven Community School, Peacehaven

The Girl

She looks, she stares, her eyes stare at my face,
When she gets angry her eyes flame up hot,
I don't like her, which fills me with disgrace,
She treats me like I belong in a cot,
Go away, go away, I shout, I shout,
I deserve to be treated with respect,
Even in truth, she makes me feel in doubt,
That girl is always so good and perfect,
My life is destroyed, my life has ended,
Her face, her clothes, everyone thinks she's best,
But to me she makes me feel offended,
Everyone in the world thinks she is blessed,
She looks, she stares, her eyes stare at my face,
I've moved on from this girl; I've won the race.

Kirsty Hoad (11)
Peacehaven Community School, Peacehaven

My Heart

Every Friday I sit at the bar,
Secretly admiring him from afar,
He never notices that I'm there,
I even have a lock of his hair;
My heart belongs to him.

Whenever I can I take his photo,
But when I do he doesn't know,
At six o'clock he gets home,
I stand in his garden dressed as a gnome;
My heart belongs to him.

His girlfriend I *will* become,
And to his children I will be Mum,
One day I will make him my man,
I love you so much, Stefan;
He will belong to me.

Megan Silversmith (13)
St John Fisher Catholic School, Chatham

Adventures Of Life

Forget the sad things in the past,
The future is a mystery,
Let life take you on its adventures,
The best is yet to be,

Let life lead you,
Let your life lead you to God,
Let your life lead you to God,
Let God lead you, love you and forgive you,

Don't you worry,
Don't you flee,
Let life lead you like a buzzy bee.

Holly Weller (11)
St John's Catholic Comprehensive School, Gravesend

Imagine A Life

Imagine a life,
Where no hearts would spare.
Where whenever you feel lonely,
You know that someone is there.

Imagine a life,
Where we could all be as one.
Hold hands whatever the race,
And dance under the red-setting sun.

Imagine a life,
Where children could go to school,
And not feel undermined or bullied,
Or be classed as uncool.

Imagine a life,
Where education is free,
Learning about the future,
How great would that be?

Imagine a life,
Where smiles are never ending,
Where joy is personified,
And hearts are beyond mending.

Imagine a life,
Where the world is at peace,
Every country safe and sound,
Sleeping happily under a warm fleece.

Imagine a life,
Where society is stronger,
Fighting through every day battles,
And lives living much longer.

Imagine that day,
When this all comes true,
But to get there we need to help each other,
Each and every one of you.

Megan Branch (13)
St John's Catholic Comprehensive School, Gravesend

The Natural World

In the glorious Earth,
There is something beautiful.
Pretty creatures of life,
Frail new forms.

In the fury of nature,
There is something primal.
Deafening crack of thunder,
Heavy drumming rain.

A smoky red sky,
Dwindles into pitch black over the rooftops,
Sprinkles with stardust and the icy puff of my breath,
Sirens blare in the distance,
Where I see the scarlet sky kiss the mountain peaks,
And coloured lights sparkle for my eyes only.

Like our hearts, the plants grow and thrive with every passing day,
Under an endless Arizona sky with clouds slowly crawling across
Like fluffy white snails, almost close enough to touch
Through the thin mountain air.

As the birds swiftly set for home
And the rabbits flee,
As we sit upon this empty shore,
It's here I want to remain, forever more.

Amie Jones (16)
St John's Catholic Comprehensive School, Gravesend

Halloween

It's Halloween,
And I am at that scene,
I am knocking on door 13,
Knock, knock, knock it goes
Knock, knock, knock,
I stepped back as the door opened,
An old wrinkly lady answered the door,
And said, 'What are you here for?'
I said, 'Trick or treat,' in a faint voice,
She said, 'I don't believe in that nonsense,
Get out of my house,'
As I leave her house,
And jump into my car,
I left to go home,
It was very far.

Charlotte Higgins (11)
St John's Catholic Comprehensive School, Gravesend

Winter Adventure

Winter was dead, so was life frozen,
School and exams were over, so off the stress,
Snow gripped the campus action,
Outdoors had lost all of its attraction.

'Life in south,' someone mentioned,
Immediately gained all of our attention.
Only in study, could the mind ignore,
Cruelty of the season, keep us indoors.

Christopher Poruchnyk (11)
St John's Catholic Comprehensive School, Gravesend

Paint Me A Picture

Pain me a picture,
Paint me something without terror,
Without a drop of fear,
Clear from transgressions and plain pure white to blue,
Frontline was treacherous you don't have a clue.

Trenches weren't the best,
If you're painting the picture surely you should know the rest,
Of course you don't, you don't know anything,
'Sit down,' they say handing a cup of tea,
They haven't felt a drop of pain I've felt,
Maybe 'Sarge' was right I need to be brave, 'hide the fear'
Don't let the enemies hear,
I vividly remember the cloud was blue,
Smokey and turned black,
My heart beating to the rhythm of the clock,
Boom! My now long lost friend, is out of sight and reach,
Paint a picture of me,
But this time with a smile.
With no transgressions
A sky powdery blue
Paint me a picture with a refined reflection in peace.

Deborah Adetiba (13)
St John's Catholic Comprehensive School, Gravesend

The Other Side Of Me!

Sometimes I'm bad, sometimes I'm nice and kind,
But sometimes you don't want to get too close.
When I'm angry, I feel pain from the painful words you say,
You walk away.
I'm criticised and mad,
But don't want you to feel the same.
You see pain and realise how you make others feel and you disappear, but the next day I feel the same.

Daniels Puzina (13)
St John's Catholic Comprehensive School, Gravesend

Smelly Spirits!

I guess I've always seen them, these ghosts are all around.
I'm never alone, although they never make a sound.
The one today was different, he seemed quite angry and cross.
He made things move around my room and acted like my boss!
He won't be here forever, they never stay that long,
I hope this one goes soon, because he leaves a nasty pong!
I'm never scared or frightened, because they never do me harm.
I even like to watch them as most are full of charm.

Annaleise Jones (11)
St John's Catholic Comprehensive School, Gravesend

Football

He strikes, he scores; 1-0
You hear the crowds roar,
Front flip, back flip, he is down on the floor,
His teammates come running, their faces in awe.

Watching the fabulous game,
This is how they make their fame,
Glorious chances were squandered,
The crowds' minds have wandered.

Will they lose? Will they draw?
Hear the crowds disheartening boos!
Cheering them on
The game must go on.

Goal! It's 2-0!
It's been such a thrill!
They have won the title!
This game has been so vital!

Callum Coombs (11)
St John's Catholic Comprehensive School, Gravesend

The Hero In The 'Knight'

He walks in peoples' shadows, he haunts the night,
Giving the evildoers a whale of a fright.
He stands in the dark, standing stouthearted.

He stands for the people in this city, making sure it doesn't drown,
He looks over this city, making sure no one takes the evil villain crown.
When there is any sort of crime,
And the police can't get there in time
This hero will save the night.

He serves justice on a plate.
Makes sure the thugs meet new cellmates.

When the sun is low and the moon is high,
He comes to peoples' cries.
Conflicted he feels. Justice he seeks
He keeps looking after this city as the day turns into weeks.

Sometimes bank vaults just aren't holding,
Evil villains keep on laughing
Ripped skin his bone is showing,
But yet he still keeps on going.

As he puts on his mask, shows his cape
Batman thinks to himself . . .

I'll make sure this city's safe.

Abdul Muhaimen (13)
St John's Catholic Comprehensive School, Gravesend

I Miss You

How many different ways can I miss you?
Wondering whether you hear my thoughts and miss me too.
We were so close,
Always together.
The bond we have nothing could sever,
I hear your laugh in my head,
So many words that will never be said,
You were so strong,
The voice that was heard,
Now there's silence, not even a word.
I look up to the sky to see you there,
The memory of losing you is a pain I cannot bear.

One day we will be together again,
For this I am sure,
There is nothing I could want more.
For now we must remain apart,
But you will always be in my heart,
The days will pass by,
The world will turn,
The only question left I ask is why, Lord, why?

Eleanor Lily Fuller (13)
St John's Catholic Comprehensive School, Gravesend

Powerful But Gentle

The very same water that carried the ark,
That houses the whale, the fish and the shark,
That sank the Titanic in oceans so cold,
Home to the young, the ancient and old.

It tosses great ships and breaks them in two,
It takes lives away with its deep grip of blue,
While calmly it stops, then, off it goes,
To foam at young feet and tickle small toes.

Whales swim, along with turtles,
Swordfish fight, and a great white hurtles,
After fish and things of that kind,
While dolphins leap leaving nothing behind.

The mother of many, holds in its grip,
The lost and the sunk, grown useless, yet, do not slip
From the great coral reef that are seen from space,
Yet hides many secrets that are too far to chase.

It gives us freedom, it keeps us all free,
It keeps the best till last for all we can see,
But it housed many creatures so long ago,
It's all still a mystery until the end of the show.

Its domain is all over, it's claimed it all,
It has taken the mountains, no matter how tall,
Its name is 'The Ocean', 'The Sea' or 'The Deep'
And in all its great glory it still does not sleep.

Jessica Austin (12)
St John's Catholic Comprehensive School, Gravesend

The Trench

The trench is like a dirty drain,
The smell's so bad it's insane,
Buried deep below the ground,
The gunfire makes the only sound.

Surrounded by a wall of mud,
The surrounding Germans make a thud,
The muddy soldiers slowly die,
The depressed ones merely cry.

Every night as I go to sleep,
I hear my fellow soldier weep,
I hear him always muttering,
I try to tell him to stop, but it's so cold I'm always stuttering.

I remember the posters they showed laughing and beer,
But all I'm feeling now is fear,
All my country want is power,
And they will not make this my last hour.

Harry Kanda (12)
St John's Catholic Comprehensive School, Gravesend

Untitled

Almost as long as there has been life, war has been a part of it.
Mankind continues to wage war even though the consequences often breed nothing else but misery.
However, when a woman is called to take responsibility of his or her country or to protect other defenceless others, a war between two countries take place!

There is no question that there is evil in the world and we must not rest on our laurels and say it is none of our business.
We cannot stand by and watch while others are being persecuted.
It is the duty of mankind to make sure that everybody is to uphold justice.

Joshua West (12)
St John's Catholic Comprehensive School, Gravesend

War Cry

My heart thunders out of my chest,
My hands are throbbing and sweaty,
Rats are viciously chewing my boots,
Goose bumps pop up on my arm as I shiver and tingle,
And the hairs on my exhausted legs stand on end,
This is it, no going back, my first day at war.

The glorious morning sun penetrates our dismal hole in the ground,
The General rouses us up, barking and shouting at his men,
His voice as loud as a group of trumpeting elephants,
I am awake now and this is World War One.

I groan and grasp as I fumble around and collect my battle gear,
The new army coat which covers me well,
But my frozen body eats up all the warmth it generates,
An old and battered mask, just in case,
It is damaged and to be honest that scares me.

Lastly, I pick up my long, sleek but dangerous gun and several rounds of bullets,
My bullet belt is wrapped tightly around my waist,
I am so terrified words cannot explain my fears and feelings right now.
That was this morning when my stomach only had gentle butterflies,
But now I am experiencing what feels like dragons dashing about inside me,
My fears have reached maximum point.

We all stand in two straight lines, in alphabetical order,
I am Michael Wallace, so I am towards the back,
The General and another smart-looking officer stand facing the lines,
Bellowing out orders and details of our cunning plan.

But I am not listening to him
Nor am I aware of the piercing silence of the men around me
I am thinking of home, the smells and warmth
The joy that sings throughout
I miss everyone so much . . .

Emily Woolley
St John's Catholic Comprehensive School, Gravesend

Untitled

My dream to win gold,
To be the best at my sport,
Hold up the flag,
Win trophies on my shelf.

The colours of nations,
Display in the rings,
Crowds of people cheering,
Calling my name,
One day my dream will come true.

Jubril Adesigbin
St John's Catholic Comprehensive School, Gravesend

War

War is prison,
If you don't make the right decision,
It drives you insane,
But you will get instant fame.

The guns are death traps,
The barbed wire only seen on a map,
The war is won,
Everything is done.

Luke Wilson (12)
St John's Catholic Comprehensive School, Gravesend

THE WAR

Men are dying.
Hitler is fighting.
Waiting for friends to return.

Rum my warmth for the night,
Wrapped around my body holding it tight,
Never escaping this dreadful sight.

Men are dying,
Hitler is fighting,
Waiting for friends to return.

Blood runs like tears from my eyes
And puddles at my feet,
I wonder how I sleep.

Men are dying.
Hitler is fighting.
Waiting for friends to return.

Waiting for the misery to die,
Will men be surviving?
Will Hitler be dying?
Will my friends ever return?

Dhrue Raja
St John's Catholic Comprehensive School, Gravesend

What Is Society?

What is society?
Is it where only beauty matters?
Where all the things you have hoped to be, shatters?
Like glass broken into a thousand pieces,
The thought of only beauty increases.
All those lies behind those pretty faces,
The truth behind that beauty it replaces.
No size zero, or that perfect height,
You're unhappy because you're not light.
Beauty and love you can't always seize them,
Some decide suicide is a way of freedom . . .
. . . You're the beautiful one, it's society who's ugly.

What is society?
A random act of kindness?
Or being the richest, making you timeless?
Fake, fantasy, fame and fortune that is all we want,
Some get nothing while the others vaunt.
Money is a thing we can't live without today,
Rules and regulations making everyone obey.
We make mistakes so we learn from it,
That's why there is courage so we commit.
Talent is what we should really appreciate,
The dollars and status we should depreciate . . .
. . . I mean can money buy you happiness?

So what is this thing we call society?

Arina Rai (15)
St Lawrence College, Ramsgate

The Second Start

The youth of today will have nothing to say,
Sitting around in prison,
Skipping school and smoking tall,
They steal throughout their lives.

On the dole to carry on and feed the healthy lifestyles,
Council houses and pregnant women to really clean it up,
She came along with wings not gone
As a saviour from Heaven.

Bearing much knowledge
And with a hand to college,
I soon was earning money
With the children not gone and Mum not done.

We started a happy family,
With money to live
And gifts to give,
Margaret had saved us and our bunny.

My children now knew the story,
Now, leave us without the trouble,
To reach out and care for those not there
And maybe it will help you.

Harrison Smith (13)
St Lawrence College, Ramsgate

The Youth Of Today

The youth of today think that we never get old,
We are smart, we are clever, and we never get bald.

We text hundreds of messages, day in and day out,
We are different from our parents there is no doubt.

We play games on iPad; we talk on the phone,
By doing all this we never feel alone.

We have hundreds of friends on Facebook and Twitter,
The boys are jewels, the girls are glitter.

We love to explore places, and riding new bikes,
We readily accept challenges, this is our psyche.

The boys want to be good at football and cricket,
They don't want anyone to take their wicket.

The girls want to be models and awesome stars,
So, they will have lots of money and flashy cars.

We drink Coca-Cola, we eat fast food,
We are young and happy, innit, dude?

Yet, deep inside . . .
I still feel the motherly touch in me,
I still feel the fatherly concern in me,
I still feel the teachers preaching in me,
I am the link between you and me.

Atharva Lad (12)
St Lawrence College, Ramsgate

The Future

A coral reef not in sight
No fish, nothing
The sky not blue, just grey
Just cities, the sun and the sea
The planet hot, hotter than ever.

The jungles and deserts
Dying monkeys and most things I see
Blankets of tigers and lions
Cover the cracked ground
Almost nothing left.

Crops wilted and trees
No food for us
Hardly any trees to give off oxygen
It's too hot for rain.

The polar ice all melted away
Polar bears and penguins
Drifting away on stranded ice.

Boom! Another nuclear weapon
World War Three!
You always hear the drumming of guns
Crash! Another bomb!
The frail planet being destroyed.

The planet is nothing now
There is no hope!
Because we destroyed it!

Hannah Cheesemore (13)
St Lawrence College, Ramsgate

Our Youth Of Today . . .

What has happened to a conversation face to face?
Our children living in a virtual world,
A silent generation, children's laughter replaced with the buzz of an electrical device,
Faces hidden in hoodies, the constant fear of crime and riots,

Bullies and racists haunt their victims destroying their childhood
Leaving them living in the shadows of fear,
Cyber bullying judging people on their backgrounds, their appearance or even the way they talk,
These little things make a person; they make us individual and interesting,

Plastic surgery changing who we are, unrecognisable faces
God made us this way, there's no need for change,
Girls desperate to be thin like the airbrushed models on our screens,
Breathing the wrong message to girls,
Encouraging bulimia, anxiety, low self-esteem and anorexia,

Our ice caps still melting, our wildlife slowly disappearing,
What would our world be without the beauty of nature?
A world without colour, without the sweet soft sound
Of the birds in the early morning,

Frustration and neglect flows through our streets,
The place we call home,
Before the dawn of a new generation will begin, what will the world be like?
We can only hope, hope,
Hope that the world will be a better place.

Olivia Keel (16)
St Lawrence College, Ramsgate

What Our Parents See But We Can't!

Why can't we see what our parents want us to see?
We're ignorant, obnoxious, arrogant and full of pride,
They plead for our cooperation but we stamp on it,
Take the other road and come back asking for help.
They'll say, 'I warned you.'

'I warned you not to cheat!'
'I warned you not to go out with him!'
'I warned you not to sleep with him!'
'I warned you to focus on your exams!'
'I warned you to tell the truth!'

We all look back on that day saying,
'They really did warn us but why didn't we listen?'
'Why didn't we just read instead of party?'
Then we'd say,
'Because we're teenagers living up to our youth.'

We were stupid, young and blissful,
But we were teenagers
Our parents were wise, but how could we know?
We were teenagers living on the edge.
Our ignorance was bliss; drinking, smoking and acting cool.

Breaking our parents' rules.
But we were young and foolish,
What if we mess up again?
We all know that we can't say that now
Our youth came and went.
Just like our mistakes.

Tomife Laniyan (13)
St Lawrence College, Ramsgate

Doorway To The Soul

A person's eyes do hold inside
The captured essence of their mind.
A spark that shows: their dreams, their hopes,
Their loves, their hates and fears.
A snatch of flame their souls light
Within those glistening pools.
A doorway to another's soul, that lets you truly see,
Our inner most thoughts and moralities.
Those churning orbs of kindred light,
The good or bad that's held inside.

Were you ever to take the time
To gaze intently into mine,
What I wonder would you find?
A bitterness or perhaps a fear
Of losing someone I hold dear?
A growing sense of wasting time?
An intensity deep down inside?
A thirst for knowledge or caring side?
Those I've loved or those I've lost?
Sadness or happiness?
What I've done or what I've not?

I hope one day that mine will be
Without that shade of melancholy.
That wizened look that does show,
I've seen more than I care to know.
I hope one day that they will show,
A clearness and purity
A good and caring soul.

For gaze into another's eyes
And you shall see their soul.

Natasha Harrison (16)
St Lawrence College, Ramsgate

Better Stop And Think Before It's Too Late!

The precious giant pandas only live in the wilderness for less than 15 to 20 years due to lack of bamboo sticks obtainable.

What's the reason, what's the reason?
Who is to blame, who is to blame?

The beautiful green forests are decreasing every year; it's making it harder and harder for petite creatures to survive.

What's the reason, what's the reason?
Who is to blame, who is to blame?

The angelic polar bears of the Arctic have no escape from the separation of the rapidly melting ice.

What's the reason, what's the reason?
Who is to blame, who is to blame?

The conspicuous landscapes are constantly being turned into fields of wind turbines,

What's the reason, what's the reason?
Who is to blame, who is to blame?

The magnificent snow leopards are agitated to find food in the cold unmerciful winter.

What's the reason, what's the reason?
Who is to blame, who is to blame?

The fluttering of colourful birds' wings is at a state where they could be no more,

What's the reason, what's the reason?
Who is to blame, who is to blame?

Bhawana Paija (14)
St Lawrence College, Ramsgate

The Heart's Saving Grace

A simple-minded fury
A lover's tear of joy
An anger of the ages
The world will destroy.

A wrath of God almighty
A cry of pain or fear
A crashing of a soldier
No one else to hear.

A dying man in trouble
A cornered victim's scream
A death to last through hist'ry
The whole world agleam.

A reigning monarch powered
A tyrant overthrown
A disaster-stricken land
A bitter wind blown.

A place to let your heart rest
A mem'rable embrace
A kiss that lasts a lifetime
The heart's saving grace.

Andrew Watson (16)
St Lawrence College, Ramsgate

Silence

Soon there will be silence.
No leaves to fall off trees.
No ferocious roars from white lions.

Seas will be calm and dead.
Just like the rest of the world,
There's just nothing left.

We don't think, we don't try
And soon we'll all die.

Catherine Dahms (12)
St Lawrence College, Ramsgate

Global Warming

The ice caps are melting
The polar bears are drowning.

The atmosphere is decaying,
The birds are falling.

The forests are burning,
The trees are suffering.

The ocean is warming,
The fish are boiling.

The planet is dying,
We aren't helping.

Jonty Tofte (12)
St Lawrence College, Ramsgate

Over

As the dust flew across the road,
Obscuring my vision,
I felt safe within the armoured bubble,
Yet my safety was not certain.

Hot red flames ate at my skin,
Causing irreplaceable damage.
Above the pain, my right leg was feeling thankfully numb,
My life had changed forever.

Scar face, ugly, 'Ew! Look at that mummy.'
They don't understand the pain I've endured and am still enduring.

My face is evidence of the world's suffering.
My leg is evidence of the lives lost.
I gave my everything; now I'm being rejected by the ones I love.
Constantly insulated and isolated.

For their freedom I lost everything . . .

Robert Mills (17)
St Lawrence College, Ramsgate

The Aurora Borealis

There I was standing on the edge of an Arctic apocalypse
The centre of the northern hemisphere
All around were waves of wondrous light
They were dancing, performing a gentle production in the sky
Sat in the middle of nothing, just the sound of the wind
Howling like a pack of wolves.

They were beautiful, nothing like I've ever seen before
Surrounding the sky in a green band, floating on a black screen
A rare occasion for only some of the luckiest people on Earth
A complete three hundred and sixty degree view
A panorama of complete amazement
To top the experience a star shooting across the sky.

The bitter wind was penetrating all seven layers of Arctic clothing
My toes, slowly losing all feeling in them
Tingles of both awe and chill ran down my spine
Every sense in my body was telling me to leave but,
A sixth sense told me to stay and admire the dancing beauty all around
Eventually though one man can only take as much pain as he can dare to.

Daniel Goodwin (17)
St Lawrence College, Ramsgate

Education

If, in our life we remain uneducated
There is neither success nor hope.
Our Lord Christ taught His 12 disciples,
Improved and educated them
And look!
What have they become?
The most important part of humanity on Earth.
Will you ever become one?

It is said that anyone can steal your possession,
But they can't steal your mentality,
It is said that anyone can make their dream come true,
But only if they have education.
If you don't have any education
What will you do with your life?
Will you succeed or struggle in your nightmare?
What if your nightmares became reality?
What will you do then?

Smriti Rai (16)
St Lawrence College, Ramsgate

My Great Grandfather

My great grandfather was put in a tank
And was made to fight on the left flank.
This Titan stood in the air 100ft tall,
Everyone was certain it would never fall.

Neither gas nor bullets could stop the metal beast,
At not one point did the fighting ever cease.
And finally in a flurry of violence the beast fell,
In this moment the beast gave a final defiant yell.

With fire red like blood, the tank was set ablaze,
With an overpowering charcoal haze.
The flames were dancing on the tank now,
He survived but you may ask how?

From the tank like a ragdoll he was flung
And in the process bitterly lost a lung.
He struggled out with a cry of pain,
Fifty years later he died, but not in vain.

Edward Prophet (15)
St Lawrence College, Ramsgate

Our Fault!

What will happen to the Earth in a few years' time?
Feels like us humans created a crime,
What can we do to fix this disaster?
We have to think about it a lot faster.

We need to stop so the temperature doesn't rise,
Before the time quickly flies,
Polar bears are in danger too,
Let's help them before there's only a few.

Walking or cycling is better than driving a car,
You can save a lot of pollution by far,
The ozone layer is getting thick,
We better do something quick!

Simran Thapa (14)
St Lawrence College, Ramsgate

A Change In The Climate

The climate is changing,
The Earth is warming,
Habitat decreasing,
We are polluting.

How can we change our way of life?
Don't just stab it with a knife.
We need to change what we do.
You can make a difference too.

Animals dying because of us,
They should be able to win our trust.
Different environments near and far
Some to them may leave a scar!

Why can't we think of someone else?
Someone that isn't just ourself,
There's others living in this place,
Everything seems to be a case.

This should not happen,
What is going on?
Climate change is serious,
Don't be delirious.

Charlotte Wayman (12)
St Lawrence College, Ramsgate

Mother Nature

Our world is always changing
Constantly rearranging.
Building houses here and there,
Eventually it'll be everywhere.
No clean air to breathe or green parks to see,
Just imagine how our world would be?

Mother Nature tells us stories of our past,
She tries to teach us how to last.
But sometimes we humans do not understand
That we are destroying her perfect land.
We do not appreciate this world of ours
Sooner or later we'll see no stars,
Due to all the pollution and troubles we cause
It's time to rewind and press pause.

We must remind ourselves of our past
Take things slow and not too fast.
We must preserve the beauty and the land
And become Mother Nature's helping hand.

Prerana Gurung (15)
St Lawrence College, Ramsgate

The Storm

In a storm there is a crack of the thunder
And the flash and the dash of the lighting.

In a storm there is the dripping and the clicking of the rain.
The howling of the gusty wind.

In a storm there is the screaming and whining of the babies.
The sound of water dripping and dropping in the puddles.

In a storm there are flashing of hazard lights on cars.
The sound of the loud hooting horns.

Kai Shadforth (13)
Seaford College, Petworth

Sounds Of Music

I hear musical images in different sounds,
Made by us all around,
A dripping tap becomes a beating drum
Leading on an army, here it comes.

Stomping feet marching on the ground,
Is a very confusing sound,
For the soldiers marching, does it make me want to cheer,
Or make me quiver with silent fear?

A child dropping marbles onto the floor,
Sounds like guns firing in the midst of war,
A trumpet playing in our school hall,
Is the soldier calling on the field to all.

But then I hear a soothing sound,
The wind making leaves swish along the ground,
So now I feel quiet and warm,
Drifting from the violet storm.

Music is the joy of life,
From when the sun rises to the dead of night,
So if you open your mind and let the sounds flow,
The music can take you wherever you want to go.

Nell Chadwick (11)
Seaford College, Petworth

The Sun

The sun, the flaming orb;
The king of our solar system,
Encircled by the worshipping planets,
Servants of the sun, trapped by gravity,
In a never-ending orbit of their powerful lord,
Its glowing light shining on the dark heavens,
Hot as a fiery furnace, bright as a billion candles.
Bringing life to our humble planet,
Seen from afar, the yellow sphere of glory,
The symbol of hope to everyone.

Alex Titcomb (11)
Seaford College, Petworth

My Great Loves

(Inspired by 'The Great Lover' by Rupert Brookes)

These I have loved;
The sourness of lemons and their tangy taste;
My feet sinking into the wet sand as the waves roll back;
The smell of freshly cut grass;
The roar of an F1 engine as it races past;
The puzzling effects of optical illusions;
The sweetness of freshly picked strawberries;
The comfort of home;
My dogs' excitement as I walk through the door;
Dancing flames and their colour and heat;
And the smoothness of sanded wood.

Dear names,
The shattering of glass;
The ooze of caramel;
Criss-cross and spotty patterns;
The 'ting' as a club perfectly hits the golf ball;
Making the first footprint in the glistening snow;
The joy and merriness of the Christmas season;
The hidden cove of 'Petit Bot' bay;
The once-a-year film that always amazes you;
And the crackles and whizzes of sparkling fireworks;
All these have been my loves.

Jamie Wall (14)
Seaford College, Petworth

Arctic

There is a bear in me . . . Claws sharpened for slicing hide . . . A set of razor-sharp fangs for ripping flesh . . . And chewing blood-stained meat – I keep this bear because the Arctic gave it to me and the Arctic won't let it go.

There is a seal in me . . . A glistening coat of soggy fur . . . Muscular flippers ready to swim . . . My nose picks out the scent of bloodthirsty killers . . . The hunter becomes the hunted . . . But my incredible speed insures my escape.

There is a walrus in me . . . Two tusks, poised to sink into my oppressor's neck . . . I am the alpha male . . . The meat is all mine and the rest of the colony will eat what remains . . . Anyone who opposes me must die – I got this too from the Arctic and the Arctic won't let it go.

There is a whale in me . . . Titanic flippers for swimming leagues every day . . . Determination fuels my strength, my stamina . . . My journey never stops . . . I must keep swimming, manoeuvring around obstacles . . . I must become one with the icy waters that ebb and flow . . . Otherwise I won't survive.

There is a glacier in me that is called life . . . A constant movement . . . Sometimes fast, sometimes slow . . . But the glacier is always moving on . . .

Harry Wheeler (14)
Seaford College, Petworth

The Star

Stars are shiny,
Stars are bright,
Stars glitter in the night,
Give you glory,
Give you peace,
Give you light up the heath.
Candy popping sight,
Brownie smell,
Furry touch,
All is well.
Make me smile,
Make me cheer,
Make all sadness clear.

Laura Snook (12)
Seaford College, Petworth

The Cheeky Monkey

I love to see
The cheeky monkeys,
Hanging in the tree.

They swing from vine,
To vine to vine,
So gracefully all the time.

But when the spears
Come down from below,
The monkeys' tears
Grow and grow.

Why do they have to get hunted?
Why do they have to suffer?
Why can't we leave them alone?
Why?
Why?
Why?

Harry Murray-Jones (11)
Seaford College, Petworth

Life

Saying how, and what life is, but words are never ever enough.
Life is wonder, life is hope, life is beauty, life is fear, life is all those tears.
Life is all we could ask for, but, is never long enough.
Life can be good, life can be bad, life is something really quite mad.
You don't know what it is and where it's from.
Life is war, life is peace, life can be bad, life can be sad, life as I said is really, really mad.
It's unimaginable, unbelievable, life is all you could want it to be, life is really my cup of tea.
Life is how we think and see, life lives beyond the sea, life you see is what you'll be.
So make the most of it when you can, think of all the things you can.

James Hannington (11)
Seaford College, Petworth

The Ballad Of Crystal May

I sent her a letter inscribed on a napkin
With a smile on the napkin, with which it was wrapped in.

Through this napkin-based system I finally confessed that
I was nothing if something the least bit interested.

(And also, I feared, a slight bit obsessed,
But I decided to keep that information repressed.)

The napkin I sent next, asked her, her name,
Expecting a response that asked me the same.

She passed back her name and I snatched it with glee,
And stared at the letters that stared back at me.

It was a name that - if names were people - I would hug and kiss all day.
According to my napkin, her name was Crystal May.

Below her name was a space, resembling a pause,
And further below was a single word: 'yours?'

I sent back my name (which I shall not repeat.)
And she smiled at me and my heart skipped a beat!

(Of course, this didn't actually happen,
I'd be far more concerned with an abnormality in my heartbeat pattern.)

Oh, Crystal May, how I'd love to walk over there and put my hands into yours,
And say something stupid resulting in an awkward pause.

But it's fine because you'd laugh and look at me sympathetically,
But, of course, I'm only speaking theoretically.

And that's why we're doomed Crystal May.

You'll forever be smiling at me in my head,
And if I dream of you, it'll be the closest you'll ever come to my bed.

But I continue to converse through my napkin based instrumentality,
And we discuss matters of hilarious abnormality.

And Crystal May proved herself to be an intellectual human being,
And I considered that maybe I'd been acting arrogantly, all seeing.

And I know it sounds stupid but maybe it was meant to be,
And the world was really designed for Crystal May and me.

And if at that very point in time I had stood from my chair and grabbed her by the waist,
Would she have smiled and pressed her lips against my face?

I decided not to because that would be nonsensical and stupid.
And for it to happen would require the work of Cupid,

And every one of his cherubims,
And I wondered if these silly thoughts and stupid things

Were bothering the mind of Crystal May.
I picked another napkin and pondered what to say.

I asked how she'd feel if she was faced
With the concept of taking our relationship (founded on napkins) to a higher place.

She didn't reply until it was nearly time to go,
And I was certain it would be a soul-crushing no.

She walked straight out the door, much to my surprise,
Before anyone else on the table had started to rise.

I looked at the place, and her now empty chair
And almost at once began to despair.

But there, in her now unoccupied space,
Was something below where had once been her face.

A napkin, laid out to the side of her plate,
And on it were written the words: 'That would be great!'

Ned Sanders (16)
Seaford College, Petworth

Aubade

I wake to the morning dawn,
Her sweet song mellifluous to my ear,
Her golden visage radiating from across the lawn,
Her animus could not be described by Solomon or Shakespeare.
So let me outline her for you:
She's been deracinated if she is not in Heaven;
She glimmers like the morning dew;
She sways my emotions like it's her profession.
If beauty in the world was finite,
Then she would be keeping it to herself.
I may seem a little forthright,
But, she is perfect.

My feelings for her make love a platitude,
So my heart will go on with great plenitude.

Matthew Miller (14)
Seaford College, Petworth

This Place

This place homes many creatures,
This place has many features,
This place keeps many secrets,
This place holds many colours,
This place can be small,
This place can be calm,
This place can be vicious,
This place holds the mightiest,
This place nurtures the weak,
This place makes humans seek,
The place helps make memories,
This place makes thing be,
This place is called the sea.

Jack Doe (11)
Seaford College, Petworth

The Snake

The snake, terrifyingly sly,
Could outsmart a crow.
Some constrict, others bite,
Catching their prey in the night.
Their long slender, scaly bodies
Slither silently in the night,
Towards the prey,
Towards the bite.
Fangs glistening in the night.

Ben Sturgeon (11)
Seaford College, Petworth

I Rule The Sky

I rule the skies.
I fly up high, I swoop down low,
I am tall, I am small,
I am black and grey,
I eat insects as my prey.

I rule the skies,
I am fat, I am thin,
Hear my songs in the skies,
Listen quick, you might miss them.

I am the hunter,
I am the hunted.
I rule the skies
I rule the skies
I rule the skies
I rule the skies.

Oscar Harris (11)
Seaford College, Petworth

The Park

(Inspired by 'Stormy Day' by WR Rodgers)

The sun shines down on the smiling scene
Enjoying entertaining the young,
Splattering and splashing of mud
Like carillon in sequence, giggles erupt
And roar like a wild chase; the football team cheer
And silent taunt of losing side
Delighted eyes of toddlers;
The groan of the slide when more children appear
A mother's displeasure of muddy knees;
The gaiety thickened by ice cream vans
And like a dancer, sway the trees.
A skipping rope swirls like a twister
Hooked in strict pattern;
And again the roar grows.
Teams scowl at one another
An anger furiously spills onto the pitch,
While competition arrogantly rises.
Like hands of a clock
The merry-go-round twists and turns,
Spinning out time thoughtfully.
Brains have been delighted;
Memories secured safely in the vault,
Never to steal away,
To be cherished.
For this day was special.
A gleeful gorgeous, generous day
In the park.

Jaime-Anne Pardey (13)
Seaford College, Petworth

Him

The curiosity on my arrival,
The process of getting to know me,
The beginning of a bond that will be impossible to break.

As you grow they will
Play with you,
Joke with you,
Comfort you,
You will start to know them,
Understand them.

The older you get, the closer they get.
At the same time, the harsher they get.
The unfairness of bedtimes you will cease to understand.
You will annoy each other and frustrate each other,
But you will never be angry with them.

The first time you go to the park,
The laughter is unstoppable,
The competition you have,
The drive to beat him.

Then comes the time when they are out past my bedtime.
The constant question, 'Is that the front door?'
The hollow sound of the house
As the army took him to Afghanistan.
As the course took him to London,
As the flight took him to Sydney.

Nick Rees Toca (14)
Seaford College, Petworth

The Black Riders

(Inspired by 'Black Riders Came From The Sea' by Stephen Crane.)

Black riders came from the sea.
There was a clang and clash of spear and shield,
And a clash and clash of hoof and heel,
Wild shouts and the wave of hair,
In the rush upon the wind.

The soldiers rushed out to defend the garrison.
There was a clang of the shields,
And the clash of the many swords,
But the last thing they saw, were the eyes of the black riders.
Dark eyes of the black riders, seeing revenge.

Hundreds of arrows soared at the black riders.
They smashed against their targets and slammed into their armour,
But you can't kill what's already dead,
And the desire for revenge kept them going,
And only after they killed him would they get eternal rest.

The black riders killed anyone who stood in their path.
Their maces cracked the bones,
And their swords splattered the blood onto the earth.
He was their commander and he betrayed them,
And now the coward had to die.

He was now alone, alone with the black riders.
He tried to run, but nobody escaped the black riders.
Their swords slashed at him,
And his blood dripped down onto the ground.
The black riders got what they came for, and now they were going away.

As dawn came and the sun gleamed over the compound.
There was a quack and shriek of the birds,
And a splash and splash of the waves.
The black riders were going within minutes.
In the rush upon the wind.

Peter Tutykhin (13)
Seaford College, Petworth

Silence

Silence. Lost memories. Buried. Gone. Some time they will be forgotten. Just the stones tell us the stories. That they were once there. Like us. Stories that let us laugh. Stories that let us cry. Stories that are remembered and the ones which fade away. Stories that we don't want to hear. Stories that we want to share.

All at one place. Here. Gathered in a different world. A world that we don't know. A world that we are afraid of. A world that we can't wait to enter.

This place lets us think. We look around; flowers, trees and stones. Many stones. Each one different, but yet the same.

Fog spills along the wild-growing grass and licks at the trees, providing a white grey gloom in the distance.
A slight breeze rustles through the trees and is gone.

Silence. We all have a story. We look back at the others to help us get through ours. They inspire us. They give us strength. They give us hope.

Silence. Lost memories. We want our stories to continue. We want them to matter. We want them to change. We want them to develop. We want them to proceed. We want them to end . . .

Silence. Lost memories. Buried.

It's time to leave. We can't look back forever. We all have our stories. We all want them to be heard. It's up to us if we listen or ignore and move on. We all need to move on. Every story has an end. Regardless if it's the worst tragedy, or the biggest relief. It all has to end some time. For a new story to begin. Most stories end at this place.

Silent. Lost. Buried. Gone.

David Smith (14)
Seaford College, Petworth

Only A Boy

He was still only a boy,
Who kept a picture to his chest,
Of his father not forgotten,
Though they are kept apart.

He was the boy that played with soldier men,
And ran with a bomber plane in his hand.
Now he wears the uniform,
And holds the gun;
Killing other men was what he was called to do.

He had signed under aged,
And fought for the freedom of many.
He hoped for pride and glory.
The boy died in the early morning,
As a man.

Mairi Donaldson (14)
Seaford College, Petworth

Friendship

Friendship is a safe house made of glass and steel.
It shelters you and holds you until the storm is over.
It is a way of expressing how you really feel.
And, when harsh words are spoken, it provides the cover.
It helps you return from the depths of your despair.

Suddenly the safe house becomes the devil's lair.
The glass is shattered by the speech of a careless word,
And it is now that you realise you're on your own again.
Now the tears are falling, your vision is being blurred;
You never thought it could cause you so much pain.

But then, the storm is over; a rainbow appears.
Someone is there to comfort you; their arms hold you tight.
Now there is a person to help you dry your tears.
The thunderstorm is over now; here comes the light.
Friendship is a blessing; it can also be a curse.
In the end it shapes you for better and for worse.

Callum Easton (13)
Seaford College, Petworth

The Ocean

In the deep of the night,
As the stars and the moon bathe in their mirror,
The ripples and waves elegantly dance,
Midnight brings tidal peace and tranquillity
To the dark and beautiful waves,
Falling and leaping, falling and leaping,
As they travel through the night.

Underneath the surface,
Is a vast living world,
The ocean is still thriving,
With creatures gliding and swooping and hunting.

Through the darkness, the moray glides,
Its long green body diving and swooping,
Like a kite takes to wind;
It slices and dashes and darts and whips,
It pounces and grabs and crunches and tears apart
Its prey.

Emerging from the surface of sandy floors
And rocky stronghold,
The octopus camouflages itself into the dark ocean blue,
Finding new strength in the cloak of the night,
Stretching and bending its flexible body
To dart down and hone in on its dinner.

So next time when you're sailing out on the ocean blue,
With the waves lapping, and the moon shining,
Look down at the waves
And think of the morays gliding, and the octopuses hunting,
And remember that the ocean is living all the time,
That the natural world never stops, but is always on the prowl,
No matter how beautiful it may be.

Daniel Low (14)
Seaford College, Petworth

Brother

This face is not recognisable to me;
The emptiness clouds your eyes.
No sound or echoes trail from your mouth.
Only so many years ago.

Youthful and strong, you continued
Into a new place filled with strangers.
This new place gave you skill and also heartache,
But improved you even still.

Older you grew and less you took,
Your mind began to crease from stress.
Along came the one girl that would make you change
Forever; she made you change.

This sadness is not recognisable to me.
This emptiness clouds your words.
Only a few words do you ever speak now,
The brother I miss so much.

When Dad left, you knew why
Before any of us, you knew why
The past has gone and done, what it has done.
Even so, you can't forget it.

If only you could get better,
The brother I miss so much.
This depression overcomes you
And overcomes us too.

Alexandria Ivy White (14)
Seaford College, Petworth

The King Of The Sea

The king of the sea,
Crowned with krill,
Enthroned by the ocean,
The dominant sea creature,
Bigger than all,
Rules the oceans;
The great blue whale.

Josh Harry (11)
Seaford College, Petworth

What Is Love?

Is love the river that never runs dry?
Is love the limit beyond the sky?
Is love the day I finally die?
What is love?

Is love a bright colour, really, really bright?
Is love a famous star, shining in the night?
Does love fix broken hearts and give them light?
What is love?

Is love a poem that reaches your heart?
Is love a fight that rips people apart?
Is love music, drama or art?
What is love?

Is love a spirit that never dies?
Is love for your heart, your brain or your eyes?
Is love the competitor, fighting for the prize?
. . . No, love is all around.

Hannah Wardrop (12)
Seaford College, Petworth

The Hunt

A brave shadow leans upon the crack of a rock,
Eyes darting from left to right, wildly,
Bright and red,
Thirsty for blood.

A dense sheet of darkness is broken by a howl,
Shrieking, screaming, growling, wailing,
A shadow swipes the floor.
More now –
Racing, chasing, pounding, sprinting.

A scampering shadow crosses the rock,
And, by the swish of a tail, the hunt was off.
Rustling through the pine trees
Leaping, shoving, panting, zooming,
Dodging all the obstacles.

When, at last, the full moon reflects onto the clearing.
The action paused,
The deer was cornered,
Panting, faster and faster,
Looking for an exit,
Looking to escape from the scene.

The wolves drew closer,
Pace by pace,
Padding lightly through the snow.

He pounced.
Grasping the deer's neck in his gaping jaws,
Biting down harder and harder, deeper and deeper,
The pack moved in.
Padding through the snow, proudly, the pack left satisfied,
The blood poured down from their sharpened teeth to their fur.

The deer was dead.

Mattie Hansing (13)
Seaford College, Petworth

Figure In The Dark

The terror of my future lies before me
Who knows what sights I'll see?
They keep telling me it's for my country,
But that's not what's bothering me.

My hopes, my dreams, my future,
It's now, not never, son.
Go over the top, get shot, get drowned,
Just don't hide away or run.

My images now are churning,
In my mind they'll never leave.
The penetrating body of gas is coming,
It's getting hard for me to breathe.

Hard pellets of rain are sinking,
Deep into the ground.
They make a mark, they hurt, they cry,
But still don't make a sound.

'It's nearly over!' my comrades cry
'We've really made our mark!'
But yet, I can't – I won't – forget,
That figure in the dark.

His grey suit, his black moustache,
His family and his wife.
He had dreams too, he hurt, he cried
And I just took away his life.

Daisy Hanbury (14)
Seaford College, Petworth

Death

Death is the most feared thing on Earth.
He takes many forms, but he's always there, at your shoulder, waiting for your time to come.
He always waits for you; even if it takes 1,000 years he will come;
As tall as the tallest man, as thin as a rake;
His cloak as black as night itself and as long as a tree.

His body of rotting flesh shows bone beneath it, shows how the maggots crawl along his bony face.
But he has no face, just a black spot waiting to be filled.

His scythe is taller than him, the blade stained red with blood, slowly dripping off.
It gives the power to control how we die, he chooses how we go.

Death serves no one. He is a law unto himself, he merely collects the dead for Heaven or Hell.
He watches our entire lives, deciding whether we've been good enough for Heaven.

He's simply there by you, watching; waiting to engulf you in his cold, dead hands.
If you look around your house or bedroom at night and your eyes start to sting only in one place that's him.
You can't see him, but he sees you every day and night.

Only when you're about to die can you see him, and only then for a brief moment.
And, when you do, he enjoys taking your soul away from the world.
Growing ever more hungry for humans, his little puppets to play with.
When you say, 'I think someone walked over my grave,' that's him.
Standing over your cold rotting corpse.

You can't run.
You can't hide.
You can't escape the immortal, Death.

Charlie Young (13)
Seaford College, Petworth

Snow

The crispy white blanket,
Engulfing nature's greenness,
Leaving behind a crystal whiteness.

As snow's fragile crust is broken
By the innocent playful boy,
The sound of crumpled paper
Nourishes your frozen ears
With happiness and warmth;
Crackling, crunching, crushing.

The screaming, the laughter of children,
The crumpling of snowballs being compacted
Ready for war.
Then the silence . . . the wait . . .

Suddenly the blistering, burning balls
Are thrown and again the happy laughs of children
Roar through the hard grey sky.

But their happiness is short lived,
For tomorrow the lush white soft powder will start to recede,
Temperature will rise, while the sun awakens,
Evaporating the evidence of battle.

Then it is gone!

Josh Medley (14)
Seaford College, Petworth

Owl In The Night

I love to see owls in the night,
In the dark, away from the light,
Below their tree is my favourite place,
Cold and dark, far, far from the human race,

Owl flying, owl hooting, that's my place to be,
Owl sleeping, owl eating, such a mystery,
Owl in the night and owl in the day
Owl still manages to find his way,

Owl swooping, gliding and ready,
Talons out and keeping steady,
Eating rodents, such as mice,
But owls finds them truly nice,

Why nocturnal, why oh why?
In the night is when they fly,
Gleaming feathers, clean and fluffy,
Always soft and never scruffy,

I love to see owls in the night,
In the dark, away from the light,
Below their tree is my favourite place,
Cold and dark, far from the human race.

Anya Ormrod Davis (11)
Seaford College, Petworth

A Year

Spring
Blossom on the trees,
Children laughing in the fields,
Spring finally came.

Summer
The sun has come out,
The grass is now green and lush,
Smell of suntan cream.

Autumn
Rustling leaves near,
Hibernating animals,
Trees losing their leaves.

Winter
The snow is falling,
Our cheeks are rosy red,
Whilst our hands are warm.

Amelia Allen (11)
Seaford College, Petworth

Rule

I rule the ground,
I am never ever found,
Because I am so feared,
Everyone shares their tears.

I can run long,
I can run short,
I can be gone,
Or I can be the sport.

I can be dangerous,
I can be shameless,
I can come last,
Or I can be fast.

I rule the ground,
I am always found,
And because I am so loved,
I can fly like a dove.

Kofi Atkinson (11)
Seaford College, Petworth

Lion

The air is thick with the smell of heat.
As a shadow stalks its prey.
As silent as space.
As cunning as fear.
Will it succeed today?
A shadow that is walking.
A shadow that is stalking.
A shadow that is hungry for blood.
Eyes burning bright.
In the dark of the night.
On a baking shell of solid mud.
Silently sneaking getting closer and closer.
And then;
It pounces, leaps, flies, its inspiration never dies.
The air is thick with the smell of heat.
As a shadow stalks its prey.

Oliver Hodkinson (11)
Seaford College, Petworth

Team

Sprinters are speeding around the track,
Distance runners are running back and forth around in circles,
Hurdlers jumping high off the ground,
People throwing javelins like Zeus throws lightning bolts,
People working together like a colony of ants,
Together everyone achieves more.

The whistle is blown, off they go,
Battling hard to win the game,
She shoots, she scores,
Together everyone achieves more.

Sprinters are speeding around the track,
Distance runners are running back and forth around in circles,
Hurdlers are jumping high off the ground,
People throwing javelins like Zeus throws lightning bolts,
People working together like a colony of ants,
Together everyone achieves more.

Loulou Robson (12)
Seaford College, Petworth

The Four Seasons – Haiku

Summer; beach
People in the sea,
Dancing in great excitement,
As waves fall on them.

Autumn; leaves falling
Leaves falling from trees,
Trees lose their leaves for winter,
Leaves float to the ground.

Winter; snow
Birds float in white trees,
Playing with fresh icicles,
Looking at the pond.

Spring; nature
Flowers start growing,
Bunnies bouncing everywhere,
The bright sun comes out.

Freya Brazier (12)
Seaford College, Petworth

Winter Wonders

The sky doth bring forth great canvasses of white,
That glimmer and dazzle in the morning haze.
Like tiny jewels in the dim sunlight,
That sparkle and shine to show off and amaze.
The people seeing this laugh and play in glee,
Dancing on ice and creating men of snow.
From the bitterness and wet, no one does flee,
But as the sun shines, the substance starts to flow.
The faces of snowmen drip and quickly morph
From the black miles of coal to gaze of fear.
Skaters return to the safety of the wharf,
They sit and watch the snow unfreeze from their pier.
And as the sun sets to the bitter cold night,
People lie in their beds, beaming with delight.
With windows we watch winters whispering winds,
While we wear whatever's warm.
Whilst we wait, we wonder if the weather will slow,
With what was the worst winter storm.
Where we were, within warming walls, we watched winter's weather wind down.
Without windows, we wouldn't see what was winter's whitest snow on the ground.

Yolanda Gumpo (14)
Seaford College, Petworth

Hunger

Can you hear it?
The sound of children fighting,
Fighting for their life,
Their stomach so big, yet so empty;
Their mouths so wet, yet so dry.

Can you see it?
The sight of mothers crying,
Crying for their loved ones.
Their tears so wet, yet waterless;
Their love ever fruitful, yet with no food.

Can you smell it?
The smell of humanity's helplessness.
What can we do?
We think we are indomitable.
However, we are just like those children,
Helpless, hungry, left for dead.

Calum Loeffen-Ames (13)
Seaford College, Petworth

The Climb

Higher, and higher, weaker and weaker,
Each grip makes your arm burn with pain and exhaustion.
Each step takes you further toward your goal, one by one.

Then you slip, fall away from whence you were,
But determination and pride swing you back to the sheer face of fear
and jealousy.
Then the slow limb tearing torture starts again.

Experience and friendship are helping you from the bottom,
Whilst trust is holding you from tumbling back down to pain and sorrow.
Then love comes, an overhang of doubt and confidence.
The part that makes or breaks the chance of your victory.
The part where, if you fall, you have to try again and again until you succeed.

The last stretch to you goal, relief and hope,
The two things that drive you to your final goal.
The two things that drive you to the end,
To reach your goal.

You finally reach your goal,
Self-confidence, self assurance and willingness to do it again.

Charles Ghinn (13)
Seaford College, Petworth

The Tsunami

All is calm;
Children playing in the sea;
The sun beating down like liquid gold;
Waves rocking with movement of the moon.

A thin layer of wind shreds across the ocean,
Whispering past smiley faces and happiness,
Completely unaware of what is going to happen.
It's coming, get ready.

Tossing, turning, tumbling, tipping,
Spoiling, splashing, spurting, swirling
This monstrous juggernaut and frightening beast,
Destroying everything in its path.

This dangerous devil;
This terrifying nightmare;
Carrying debris in its watery clasps
Never to be seen again.

The cries of people,
The confusion and chaos,
Leaving behind death and destruction
Just one big wave.

Eva Glynne-Jones (14)
Seaford College, Petworth

Family

A family
Is made of love and tears,
Laughter and years.
It grows stronger
With the passing of time.
More precious
With the making of memories.

Sometimes a family is made of ones
You don't like for a while . . .
But you love for a lifetime.
It's a girl whose value is found
Not in numbers, but in its capacity to love.

It's the place you find
Someone to encourage you,
Believe in you.

Cian & Swapnil Jha (15)
Seaford College, Petworth

Millwall Chairman Protest Song

It's a little bit funny this feeling inside,
We're not one of those who can easily buy,
We don't have much money, but boy if we did,
We'd buy a decent player and he could score big.

If I was a manager but then again no,
Or a man who actually bought players, but never on loan,
I'd throw in my money and give it a try,
There might be a Messi or a Beckham we'd buy.

I hope you don't mind,
I hope you don't mind Mr John Berylson,
How wonderful Millwall could be,
If you just did one.

Kian Daniels (13)
The Leigh Technology Academy, Dartford

Alone

Have you heard the people crying?
Because they feel alone.

Have you ever felt the way your heart sinks,
When no one around you likes you?
Or when you try to fit in,
But you still stand out from the crowd?

Have you heard the people crying?
Because they feel alone.

If you close your eyes and look closely,
Then you will see all the memories you have put in me.
It makes me feel sad, angry and alone.

Have you heard the people crying?
Because they feel alone.

I feel so alone like a bird who cannot fly,
Like a daisy in a field of tulips.

Have you heard the people crying?
Because they feel alone.

I feel like I am being stuffed down the belly
Of a treasure chest and being locked away forever.

Have you heard the people crying?
Because they feel alone.

Charlotte Baker (12)
The Leigh Technology Academy, Dartford

Girls Of The Taliban

Girls of the Taliban, taking no more,
It's not right, there should be a new law,
Girls and boys should learn together,
Girls should have rights forever and ever.

Independence is all they desire,
They can't read or write,
They stay out of sight,
So they think this is right?

Girls of the Taliban taking no more,
It's not right, there should be a new law,
Girls and boys should learn together,
Girls should have rights forever and ever.

Working in the household with mother and baby,
Education is all they admire,
Whilst the Taliban cause destruction and fire.

Girls of the Taliban taking no more,
It's not right, there should be a new law,
Girls and boys should learn together,
Girls should have rights forever and ever.

Ellie Taylor (12)
The Leigh Technology Academy, Dartford

The Population Of Africa: Do You Hear Them Cry?

The population of Africa, do you hear them cry?
They ask a simple question, why?
Will they live much longer,
Will they live at all . . .

Dirty water, no sanitation for every generation,
Just tinned houses packed like sardines,
What does this mean?

The population of Africa, do you hear them cry?
They ask a simple question, why?
Will they live much longer,
Will they live at all . . .

Children on the streets not even at school,
Working day in and day out with only one rule.
Scavenging like foxes, to bring back food, to lighten the mood.

The population of Africa, do you hear them cry?
They ask a simple question, why?
Will they live much longer,
Will they live at all . . .

Will they take this at all?
Will they start to break?
Lions stuck in cages,
Wanting to be freed.
To stand up for their rights,
Opening peoples' eyes and
Showing them the light.

Jessica Ritson (12)
The Leigh Technology Academy, Dartford

Lonely Streets

People always stare,
Like I'm a nobody,
People point and glare,
Don't they know I'm human?

It's like I'm a disgrace,
My family agree,
People looking down on me,
Can't they hear my plea?

Sitting on the streets,
I feel my life decay,
People say you're dirty,
Some just call me names,
They try to relate to me,
Say I know how you feel,
They don't know what it feels like,
They work behind a till.

Nobody to talk to,
When the night comes in,
Nobody to turn to,
When the day draws in.

Some give me money,
A penny or two,
Do they think that can cover,
The holes in my shoes?

Sitting on the streets,
I feel my life decay,
People say you're dirty,
Some just call me names,
They try to relate to me,
Say I know how you feel,
They don't know what it feels like,
They work behind a till.

They think I can't hear them,
Whispering ear to ear,
It's really not my fault,
I can't get a career,

When they come and get me,
I have to move away,
Constantly looking over my shoulder,
All night-time and all day.

Katie Brown (12)
The Leigh Technology Academy, Dartford

A Fight To Learn

A fight to learn,
She fought for equality for all girls
A given, for most around the world,
The right to learn, surely we deserve,
Not just a life to obey and to serve.

Such an ambition for one so small,
To fight for the rights of one and all,
To go against a belief so unjust and unfair,
To speak out when others just stand and stare.

She comes from Swat Valley, Pakistan,
An area influenced by the Taliban,
With religious beliefs harsh and extreme,
Supporting inequality, crushing women's dreams.

The Taliban warned of their extreme displeasure,
But Malala was strong, not to succumb to pressure.
In 2012 their revenge they did carry out,
A bullet to the head to put an end no doubt.

But Malala survived, and with help far and wide,
She can recover a life deserved, not denied,
But the question for all governments around the world,
Is why they were put to shame by such a young girl?

Charlotte Thom (12)
The Leigh Technology Academy, Dartford

Foxes Of Doom

Foxes are orange and furry,
And they are full of fury,
If they were in a courthouse,
They'd be convicted guilty by the jury.

They are sly and crafty,
Orange bundles of pain,
Smarter than they seem and
Relentless without shame.

If I were you, I'd watch your back;
Their brains are now mutating.
The government probably won't do much,
But on this they should be concentrating.

So keep your two eyes open
And have a Boost bar opened
Because once their reign of terror begins,
I doubt they could be stopped . . .
They are the foxes of doom.

Alex Taylor (13)
The Leigh Technology Academy, Dartford

My Maths Lesson

Bored.
I'm not going to work,
I'm just going to fiddle,
Go away.
Just don't bother,
Burn it.

Charlie Walter Asbury-Smith (12)
The Priory Coxlease School, Lyndhurst

Darkness

In the playground, the sun has fled,
The darkness is still, but it's not that you dread,
Something lurking in the dark, something not quite alive,
Waiting for the lift, but it has yet to arrive.

Encircling around me, what will be my fate?
Encircling around me, coming through the gate,
Encircling around me, seeing things I'm not,
Searching in my pockets for things I haven't got.

Senses going numb,
All the things I haven't done,
Trying to hide, nowhere to go,
Can't run from the darkness, but I wish it were so.

I see the faint glow then comes the growl,
Does it bite, does it howl?
No, it comes with rushing legs and outstretched arms,
And lots and lots of comforting bright light.

Ben Pritchard (11)
Wilmington Grammar School for Boys, Wilmington

The City

The city,
Standing there, majestically towering over all those who dared defy it,
The concrete jungle,
The crowds of people scattering around the floors of the forests like the bugs that inhabit the trees,
Helicopters hovering like the tropical birds that fly from branch to branch,
Shouting crowds bustling over the pavements,
The young and the weak being pushed from post to post,
Crying out for help, not being heard over the screams of the terrified crowds,
Those people were never forgotten, the remains of what they had lost in the wreckage,
Not undignified, neither were their memories, or their hearts.

Harry Blackley (12)
Wilmington Grammar School for Boys, Wilmington

Dyslexia

Dyslexia means 'trouble with words'
The trouble is, they're not spelt like they're heard.
I like LEGO Mindstorms, origami and buses.
But they won't help you pass eleven pluses.

So, I had to work, till almost dead,
'Find the hidden words!' they said.
'But they're all hidden! I just can't do it!
With mad words like this, I won't get through it!'

Like yacht. Why not yot?
Or why not nocht?
And why is 'though' not spelt like 'show' or 'go'?
It doesn't make sense. I really want to know.

I hate eight, it's not a great favourite of mine.
Seven isn't Heaven, but none is fine.
Why does moon not end like 'tune'?
I really hope they'll change it soon.

I worked hard and passed the test!
My tutors helped me do my best.
Now it seems I'm not a fool.
Because I'm in a grammar school.

Daniel Hudson (12)
Wilmington Grammar School for Boys, Wilmington

Seasons

New leaves and buds start to appear,
The warmer days are getting near,
Little animals start to wake,
Hibernation is about to break,
Hedgerows start to bloom,
With spring colour to brighten the gloom.

Hot summer days with long hot nights,
Colourful deck chairs and windbreaks make the beaches bright.
Ice creams are a perfect treat,
Warm grains of sand tickle your feet.

Crunch, the golden autumn leaves beneath your feet,
Their colours warm against the sky.
Days draw in, winter soon to meet.
Chestnuts hot for all to eat.
Bonfire night, the fireworks crackle and pop,
Rockets that soar begin to drop on unsuspecting passersby,
Children have fun making their 'Guy'.

Crisp, cold wintery nights,
Jack Frost came to bite.
In the dark, he laid his white,
A coat of crystals sparkling bright,
Christmas trees, holly, snow, peoples' houses all aglow.
Socks and jumpers, fires bright, make for cosy days, just right!

Finlay Cleland (12)
Wilmington Grammar School for Boys, Wilmington

Nature

Here I stand with nature's beauty in my eye,
The towering trees gently stroking the sky.

Hearing the wind whistling into my ear,
Whispering its secrets they sounded so dear.

The bluebirds were tweeting and filling the sky,
The flowers were blooming and reaching up high.

The colours were truly a sight to behold,
Rocky mountains and green lands so bold.

As I looked at the river's water, crystal clear and blue,
The blazing sun make nature glisten with a brilliant hue.

George Needham (11)
Wilmington Grammar School for Boys, Wilmington

Lion

Creeping, crawling through the night,
Some may give you quite a fright.
Sneakily stalking, watching their prey,
Some sit and wait all day.
Time passes, it has no meaning,
Watching their prey suffer with no feeling.

Keeping a watchful eye,
At everything that passes by.
A saddened look as he sits alone,
Sitting silently on his animal throne.
Off he springs jumping through the air,
Now he's gone, he is not there.

Matthew Varley (12)
Wilmington Grammar School for Boys, Wilmington

Living With Aspergers

I long to understand the big wide world.
I know I'm different from everyone else.
I try to understand what people say.
However, it's mumbo jumbo most of the day.
They call me 'ginge', they're being unkind.
It's just 'banter' everyone says,
Now everyone's laughing with the unkind people.
I laugh along louder and louder, panic starts in my stomach.
I don't get the joke.
I hope nobody asks what we're laughing about.
By the time we arrive home I'm ready to burst.
It seems my time at school is the worst.
I have held it together most of the day.
Relief at last I can hide away.
My bedroom, my palace, my safe place.
Everything safe in its proper place.
I jump on the bed and pull back the covers.
'James, James!' My peace is broken, Mum is calling me to do my homework.
Out comes my planner, I can feel the panic rise again what subject is it and when is it due.
'Please, please be maths,' I secretly whisper, the happiness I get from adding those numbers.
No, it's English, the subject I dread. They want me to write a story or
poem instead.
A long night ahead for me and my mum, she tries to help me understand things called 'feelings' and 'emotions'.
It doesn't matter disability or not, treat everyone the same.

James Town (12)
Wilmington Grammar School for Boys, Wilmington

Troubled Times

Derelict dwellings,
Burnt-out cars,
Boarded-up homes,
And empty bars.

Closed down stores,
With swaying shutters,
Streets full of rubbish,
And smelling gutters.

Empty schools,
Dark day and night,
Classrooms abandoned,
Without any light.

Factories closed,
With crumpled walls,
No workmen,
Just their tools.

Cloud winds,
Blowing signs,
Misty air,
Of troubled times.

Matthew O'Dolan (12)
Wilmington Grammar School for Boys, Wilmington

Pluto The Dwarf Planet

Pluto is the bullied child,
He sits, alone and dejected,
In the far reaches of the solar system,
On his axis, he runs around, but finds no one.

He is different, and the people of Earth have forgotten him.
He is lonely, and he observes the other planets with loathing.

He finds the bullying unbearable.
He is sniggered at, and names and taunts fly across the solar system,
Piercing his feelings like daggers.

His appearance makes him vulnerable.
His puny form scoffed upon by Jupiter and the other planets.

When a meteor hits him,
He feels great pain,
But the other planets feel nothing.

If only he wasn't so small.

He is Pluto, the dwarf planet.

Sean Lewis (12)
Wilmington Grammar School for Boys, Wilmington

In My World

The brightness is an enemy,
A villain to my eyes,
Just a reckless bully,
A killer in disguise.

A glare in my face,
A blur to my sight,
An evil embrace,
Just bring back the night.

And when my sleep comes,
The noise hurts my ears,
A rattle weighing tonnes,
It brings me to tears.

I socialise with struggle,
They stare with those eyes,
A quick and utter mumble,
And then I say goodbye.

The floor is my friend,
At least when I talk,
They want me to look at them,
But I'm not a hawk.

Do people have to stare,
As I walk through the street?
As though I'm something rare,
When I'm watching my feet.

I'm an alien to them,
Or a 'one of a kind',
Maybe a new found gem,
Or two species combined.

And now he is crying?
It doesn't make sense,
They were only words,
And hardly an offence.

But I'm not to change,
The ones who stare are,
For they think I'm strange,
But I'm just an odd star.

The brain is astounding,
They think my mind's mystic,
And all this poem does,
Is explain that I'm autistic.

Max Sheaf (13)
Wilmington Grammar School for Boys, Wilmington

Nerve Consumption

I'm writing this by force,

It's not my choice,

This 'poem' I've had to endorse,

Worst thing is, I can't make any sort of noise.

You know those days,
When you're down as hell,
Then my teacher says,
'Keep going, you're working well!'

I then think, if she's blind or cannot see,
Because I haven't even started,
Is she out of her mind?
Or is it just me?

These pesky little nerds writing away,
Showing me up with ease.
My mind has gone blank. You could say it's grey.
Ideas are what I need to succeed.

I can't even copy him, his writing's terrible, even emotional,
It's frightening, funny and fresh off the boat,
I scratch my head in confusion and think how this is even doable?
A few classmates look at me and say, 'Oh dear, look at this dope!'

I give up . . . close mind, close book and pencil case,
Sound mind, sound body they say,
But how is that possible if I can't co-ordinate?
I need to convert to a religion, so I can pray . . .

Michael Bunani (13)
Wilmington Grammar School for Boys, Wilmington

Young Writers Information

We hope you have enjoyed reading this book - and that you will continue to enjoy it in the coming years.

If you like reading and writing poetry drop us a line, or give us a call, and we'll send you a free information pack.

Alternatively if you would like to order further copies of this book or any of our other titles, then please give us a call or log onto our website at www.youngwriters.co.uk

Young Writers Information
Remus House
Coltsfoot Drive
Peterborough
PE2 9BF
(01733) 890066